International Policnomics.

What can we learn from decisions made in the past?

Antranik Artinian
Benjamin Ian Chen
Isabela de Almeida Godoy
Amy Espinoza Caldas
Júlia Felippe Goldman Vel Lejbman
David Xu

Edited by
Laura Maria Amaya Lamir

Copyright © 2023 Youth Politician
All rights reserved.
ISBN: 9798504622958

Contents

Chapter I: Africa — 9
- The Rwandan Genocide (1914) — 10
- Apartheid in South Africa (1948-1994) — 13
- The Algerian War (1954-1962) — 16
- The Second Sudanese Civil War (1983-2005) — 20
- The Angolan Civil War (1975-2002) — 23
- Boko Haram in Nigeria (2002-Present) — 27
- The Arab Spring in North Africa (2010-2011) — 30
- The Western Africa Ebola Virus Epidemic (2014-2016) — 34

Chapter II: Asia — 38
- The Chinese Civil War (1927-1949) — 39
- The Korean War (1950-1953) — 42
- The Vietnam War (1955-1975) — 44
- Japan's Lost Decade (1991-2001) — 47
- The Asian Financial Crisis (1997-1998) — 49
- The Saffron Revolution (2007-2008) — 52
- Chinese Stock Market Turbulence (2015-2016) — 54
- The Anti-Extradition Law Amendment Bill Movement (2019-2020) — 56

Chapter III: Europe — 59
- The Russo-Japanese War (1904-1905) — 60
- British Foreign Policy and Defence Strategy Post-Brexit (2016-Present) — 64

Chapter IV: Latin American & the Caribbean — 69
- The Mexican Revolution (1910-1924) — 70
- Argentinian Peronism (1946-1976) — 71
- The Cuban Revolution (1953-1959) — 73
- The Brazilian Military Dictatorship (1964-1985) — 75
- The Chilean Military Dictatorship (1973-1990) — 77

The Lost Decade (1980's)	79
The Fuljimori Dictatorship in Peru (1990-2000)	80
Latin America's 'Pink Tide' (2000-Present)	82
The Venezuelan Crisis (2013-Present)	84
Chapter V: Middle East	**87**
Sykes-Picot Agreement (1917)	88
The Balfour Declaration (1917)	90
Turkish War of Independence (1919-1923)	91
Syrian Revolt (1925-1927)	94
Saudi-Yemeni War (1934)	96
Middle East & World War II: A Summary (1939-1945)	98
Arab-Israeli War (1948)	101
Kurdish-Turkish Conflict (1978-Present)	103
The Iranian Revolution (1979)	105
First Palestinian Intifada (1987)	108
The Gulf War (1991)	109
The Oslo Accords (1993/1995)	111
Second Palestinian Intifada (2000-2008)	113
The Iraq War (2003-2011)	115
Israel's Withdrawal from Gaza (2005)	117
The Lebanon-Israel War (2006)	119
The Arab Spring in the Middle East (2010)	120
The Syrian Civil War (2001-Present)	122
The Killing of Osama bin Laden (2011)	124
Yemeni Civil War (2014-Present)	126
Killing of Jamal Khashoggi (2018)	128
Lebanon's Socio-Economic Crisis (2019-Present)	130
Chapter VI: North America	**133**
The Cold War (1947-1991)	134
Early 1980's Recession	142
The United States' S&L Crisis (1986-1995)	145
Black Monday (1987)	148
Early 1990's Recession	150

The Wall Street Crash (1929) and The Great Depression (1929-1930)	151
The Dot-Com Bubble (2000-2002)	155
9/11 and its Economic Repercussions (2001-Present)	156
Bibliography	159
Acknowledgments	172
About the Authors	175

Chapter I: Africa

Júlia Felippe Goldman Vel Lejbman

The Rwandan Genocide (1914)

What happened? Rwanda is divided in three ethnic groups: the Hutus, who represent 85% of the population; the Tutsi, 14%; and the Twa, 1%. Ethnic tensions have been present in Rwanda since its colonial period when the Belgians regarded the Tutsis as 'superior' in comparison to the Hutus and favored them by making them the ruling ethnicity, in an odd oppression of the majority by the minority.

In 1959 the Hutu (majority) raised up against the Tutsi (minority), forcing nearly 330,000 Tutsis to seek refuge in neighboring countries. After the independence in 1962, Major General Juvenal Habyarimana (a moderate Hutu and a member of the National Revolutionary Movement for Development (NRMD)) ruled the country and tensions were again exacerbated as a result of the invasion of Rwanda in 1990. The occupation was carried out by the Rwandan Patriotic Front (RPF) formed by Tutsi refugees. The government's response was to arrest some Tutsi residents suspected of involvement and, from 1990 to 1993, the fighting continued with government officials directing massacres of the Tutsi.

In 1993 a peace deal was agreed on, establishing a transition to a power-sharing government. The agreement angered Hutu extremists and tensions continued to build up until on April 6, 1994, the airplane transporting Rwandan President Juvénal Habyariamana and Burundian President Cyprien Ntaryamira was shot down. Speculations of guilt from both sides disseminated. Extremist Hutu militias, the Interahamwe and the Impuzamugambi, along with the Rwandan armed forces (FAR) started killing Tutsis as well as moderate Hutus, with extreme violence and disregard for human life.

The killings: The killings started just hours after Habyariamana's plane crashed, with Hutus militias setting up roadblocks and barricades and murdering Tutsis indiscriminately. During the genocide, ID cards contained people's ethnic groups facilitating the massacre. The bloodshed quickly spread from Kigali to other cities, with body counts increasing at a calamitous speed. Husbands killed their wives, entire families were murdered, even priests and nuns were involved in the genocide. The government also had a great deal of responsibility for the murders, rewarding killers with food, drinks, drugs and money. The radio was an important factor in encouraging ordinary people to carry out the genocide, dehumanizing the killing of Tutsis by referring to their murder as "weeding out the cockroaches". This entailed an 'ethnic cleansing' purpose, influenced by the 'Hutu power' ideology. It was also through the radio that lists with names, addresses and license plates of Tutsis were propagated. The genocide lasted 100 days and around 800,000 Tutsis and moderate Hutus were killed. Until the present day, 26% of the Rwandan population suffers from post-traumatic stress disorder due to this episode in their history.

International response: One particularity of the Rwandan genocide was how it unraveled in the media. The media covered the events live and broadcasted them throughout the world. The international community's response, however, was insufficient, lacking action. Even though UNAMIR, the UN peacekeeping force in Rwanda, was in Rwanda during the genocide, after the murder of ten Belgians the Security Council voted for the exit of UNAMIR, with the United States as the main advocate. The UN would not take action again until mid-May, when hundreds of thousands had been killed, recognizing the event as genocide and pledging to send troops. When the UN troops arrived, nonetheless, it was too late: the genocide had come to an end, leaving scars that haunt Rwandan people up to the present day. Another international response, that raises contradictory speculations, is the French intervention, approved by the UN. A former colonial power, France had several ties with different African countries and, in the case of Rwanda, was an ally of the Hutu government. The French established a humanitarian zone in southwestern Rwanda, a safe zone for Tutsis. It is believed that France helped some Hutus involved in the genocide to escape.

Developments: The Rwandese Patriotic Front, formed by Tutsis refugees in neighboring countries in 1990, resumed fighting faced with the horrors of the genocide. The civil war started and the RPF was able to gain control over Kigali, the capital of the country. Alongside the civil war, negotiations took place in Tanzania. More than 2 million Hutus fled the country to the Democratic Republic of Congo (then known as Zaire), driven by the fear of retaliation. The RPF established a coalition government with President Pasteur Bizimungu, a Hutu, and Vice-President Paul Kagame, a Tutsi. When in power, the RPF pursued Hutu militias in DR Congo and fought the Congolese army, which supported the Hutus. The fighting resulted in the RPF deposing Mobutu Sese Seko and installing Laurent Kabila as president, which then led to the first Congo War in 1996. Back in Rwanda the NRMD party, a protagonist in the organization of the genocide, was outlawed, a new constitution was ratified eliminating the reference to ethnicity and Kagame was elected to a ten-year term in the first legislative elections of the country. Kagame was elected to his third term in 2017, with a majority of 98%.

The International Criminal Tribunal for Rwanda: The International Criminal Tribunal for Rwanda (ICTR) was an international court of law established by the UN Security Council in October 1994, that had the aim to prosecute individuals involved in the genocide. The trials began in 1995, with high-rank individuals. As many suspects' locations were unknown, the prosecution process was difficult but, as of 2019, the Tribunal had indicted ninety-three individuals, convicted guilty of war crimes, act of genocide and rape. The ICTR was closed in 2014. Rwanda also dealt with the perpetrators' trials with its traditional community court system, the Gacaca court, trying more than 1.2 million cases.

What can we learn from it? The main lesson we can take from the Rwandan genocide comes from the ineffective and insufficient international response. When it comes to human rights violations and, especially, genocide and the complete disregard to human life, the international community should not hesitate in taking action. As complicated as conflicts can be, human life should never stop being a priority for the international community, despite their race, ethnicity, nationality, religion. The international human rights system should have a more effective mechanism in order to intervene in situations where human life is at risk.

Apartheid in South Africa (1948-1994)

What happened? Even before apartheid, South Africa was marked by racial discrimination and segregation inherited by its history of colonization and slavery. Although the black population represents the majority of South Africa's population, the 'white supremacy' ideology has endorsed a certain dominance by the white population, mainly Dutch-descended Afrikaners. The country's discriminatory laws, known as pass laws, go back to the 18th century and required members of the non-white population to carry identification papers and restricted their movement to certain areas. The pass laws would be exacerbated with apartheid becoming more rigidly controlled. Another important law that represents the outlining of the apartheid is the 1913 Land Act, a law that, legally speaking, marked the beginning of territorial segregation. The apartheid, however, would only effectively start after the Afrikaner National Party's won the elections in 1948. Although the apartheid, Afrikaner for 'separateness', was not so different from the already existing segregation in South Africa, it institutionalized segregation as a part of the law, separating the population based on their skin color and punishing those who disagreed. Under the false promise of equal development and freedom of cultural expression, apartheid forced the non-white population, especially black South Africans, into disempowerment, underdevelopment, poverty and violence. Apartheid's laws would remain in force for almost fifty years, being finally repealed in 1991 by President F. W. de Klerk.

Apartheid laws: These laws controlled the lives of black South Africans completely, restricting nearly every aspect of their lives. From laws regulating the movement of black people to laws prohibiting black South Africans to marry white people, the black population was denied its free will and autonomy, having their actions controlled by the state. Despite its several discriminatory laws, it was composed of a few laws that represented the pillar of the segregationist system. The Population Registration Act of 1950 determined the registration of people according to their racial group (white, colored, black, Indian or Asian). This law facilitated much of the discrimination and segregation mechanisms, since it divided the population into racial groups, in some cases even families would be divided by the law. Another structural law of apartheid was the Group Areas Act of 1950. This was the law that effectively started physical separation between races, determining the removal of groups of people into areas designated for their racial group. The Promotion of Bantu Self-Government Act of 1959 further intensified the physical separation started by the Group Areas Act. By moving black people out of the city, the law cast out the black population from urban areas, leaving a small part of South Africa to the majority of the population. The act created ten Bantu homelands or Bantustans, where the black population was excluded, removing them from the nation's political body.

Rebellions and resistance: The apartheid system was characterized by laws and measures used to demobilize and divide the non-white population in order to limit and even eliminate its political power and ability to organize social uprisings. Notwithstanding, it was also marked by rebellions and resistance. The African National Congress (ANC) embodied the most significant opponent to the regime. The initial protests against apartheid laws were led by the ANC in the 1950s and consisted of mass mobilizations that became known as the Defiance

Campaign. The Defiance Campaign was characterized by acts such as the burning of pass books, the boycott of white businesses, strikes and non-violent protests. The government responded with violence, arresting protesters based on unfair legal proceedings.

Later on, in 1960 during a peaceful protest in the township of Sharpeville black people, associated with the ANC, invited arrest as an act of resistance. As a result, sixty-nine protesters were shot and killed by the police. This episode enlightened the anti-apartheid leaders about the ineffectiveness of peaceful means to achieve their objectives. Hence, military wings of anti-apartheid groups were formed, including one of the ANC. Nelson Mandela was the founder of Umkhonto we Sizwe, the military wing of the ANC, and was arrested in 1961 accused of treason.

After the 1960 protest, the government declared a state of emergency, stiffening apartheid laws. Protests, however, continued to happen to the extent that black school children marched to protest against Afrikaans language being a requirement in June 1976. The police again met protesters with violence, massacring around 100 protesters. Following this, protest spread throughout South Africa and the international community manifested itself.

In 1973 the UN General Assembly finally denounced apartheid and later in 1976 the Security Council voted to impose a mandatory embargo on the arms' sale. Apart from that, both the United Kingdom and United States instituted economic sanctions on South Africa.

Nelson Mandela: Nelson Mandela was an important activist of the African National Congress. After being arrested and sentenced to life in prison in 1961, Mandela continued his role as an activist, trying to coordinate protests and resistance from inside the prison, as well as trying to conduct secret negotiations, which had no fruitful outcome. Nelson Mandela's arrest drew international attention and was an important factor in reviving the anti-apartheid cause, both nationally and internationally. He was finally released from prison in 1990, by South Africa's new President F. W. de Klerk, after the resignation of

President P. W. Botha in 1989. Apart from releasing Mandela, de Klerk lifted the ban from the ANC and, working closely together with Mandela himself, started negotiating a new constitution.

In 1991 apartheid was finally repealed and in 1993 both Mandela and de Klerk won a Nobel Peace Prize. Nelson Mandela became South Africa's president in 1994, under the now legalized African National Congress political party. Plus, the new constitution came in effect, officially ending the apartheid system and making South Africa a country no longer ruled by racial discrimination.

What can we learn from it? Initially, the apartheid was deceivingly portrayed as a way of promoting the development of all racial groups equally. The reality, however, was very different: principally black South Africans were pushed into a life of poverty, discrimination, lack of political participation and hopelessness. In our contemporary world permeated by social media and fake news, South Africa's apartheid teaches us that not everything is what it seems. Despite the original discourse that the apartheid would promote equal opportunities, it did the exact opposite, depriving the black population of a series of rights. What we can learn, thus, is to analyze very carefully the promises that are made to us and, mainly, to not believe in everything that we are told.

The Algerian War (1954-1962)

Colonial rule and nationalist movements: Algeria was conquered by France in 1830, thus, becoming part of the French metropolitan state. During the conquest the nation of Algeria resisted. The resistance was represented by the figure of Emir Abdelkader, the Sufi brotherhood leader, and Algerians experienced widespread violence with operations against said defiance. The colonial rule established by the French was characterized by a tradition of violence that caused the decrease of nearly one-third of the native population between the beginning of the French invasion to its conclusion in the mid-1870s.

Apart from all the violence, there was a mutual incomprehension between the colonists and the colonized. The colons were known as pied noirs ("blackfeet") and despite being the minority of the population—10% of the general populace—they enjoyed the privileges of a ruling minority while excluding Algerians from higher education, lines of communication, health services, among others. The pied noirs asked for an apartheid-like regime, with white dominance.

Although the national resistance was defeated in the process of conquering Algeria, there were other nationalist movements dissatisfied with the situation, mostly demanding basic rights. On a more conservative approach, there were the so-called assimilationists who considered permanent union with France if the Algerians were guaranteed equal rights to the French. In this same line, the Association of Algerian Mulsim 'Ulamã' (Association des Uléma Musulmans Algériens; AUMA) encouraged a sense of Muslim Algerian nationality. On the other hand, The National Liberation Front (Front de Libération Nationale; FLN) was more proletarian and radical, preaching initially for the end of Algerians' deprivation, and later on, resorting to organized violence in order to attain Algeria's independence.

The Setif massacre: The Setif massacre is an important event in the history of the Algerian war of independence. It started as a peaceful demonstration in May 1945, after the surrender of Germany in World War II. This manifestation is considered the last peaceful attempt towards independence. Algerian forces, who had fought for France in the war, displayed Algerian nationalist flags at Setif. French soldiers responded by shooting and killing several demonstrators. What followed was an unorganized uprising resulting in an estimated 100 pied noirs killed. France, then, started a violent suppression and retaliation, killing 8,000 Muslims, according to French sources, or 45,000, according to Algerian sources. Even though the war for independence would only start nine years later, in 1954, the Setif massacre is considered to be the foundation of the struggle for independence since it made explicit the inefficiency of peaceful means.

The Algerian War of Independence: November 1954 is documented as the start of the Algerian War of Independence, when the National Liberation Front (FLN) launched armed revolts throughout Algeria. Engaging in guerrilla warfare, the FLN coordinated small-scale attacks against French military posts as well as the killing of pied noirs and loyalists. The French, as it would become usual during the war, responded with extreme violence, bombing towns and villages, and arresting and torturing Algerians.

The fighting initially started in rural areas but spread rapidly throughout Algeria, reaching other parts of the country, including the capital Algiers and other urban centers. The Battle of Algiers, as it came to be known, was both a strategy to get international attention, but it also facilitated the hiding among civilians. The battle in the capital also meant higher costs for the French.

Violence skyrocketed at this time, with the FLN bombing and assassinating both French officials and civilians. Conjointly, there were massive searches, military assaults and torture during interrogations on the French's behalf. This war was defined by crude, boundless violence. The FLN recurred to guerrilla warfare's practices of, for instance, planting bombs in public venues, and France retaliated by sending troops and helicopter-bombing the opposition's territory, along with persecuting and torturing dissidents.

Endings: The first round of negotiations between the French government and the FLN began for good in May 1961. After a referendum held in January of the same year, it became abundantly clear that both mainland citizens and the Algerian population wished for Algeria's independence. Accordingly, French President Charles de Gaulle held secret negotiations in Evian with the FLN. In March 1962 in the course of a second round of negotiations, a cease-fire was declared.

The Secret Army Organization (Organisation de l'Armée Secrète; OAS), composed by pied noirs who were determined on the permanence of French rule in Algeria, employed acts of terror in order to interrupt peace negotiations. The attempt failed as members were arrested, and a truce was concluded with the FLN. It was decided that a referendum would take place in July 1962 determining whether Algeria would be independent or not. The result showed 6 million votes in favor of independence and only 16,000 against. On July 1, 1962, Algerians voted and had a say in the establishment of their independence, finally achieving the dream of an "Algérie algérienne". The next day President de Gaulle officially acknowledged Algeria's independence and signed the Evian Accords, a peace agreement with the FLN.

The war is estimated to have caused at least 300,000 deaths, although Algerian sources claim as many as 1,5 million. The conflict also resulted in the destruction of villages, devastation of forests and forced migration of 2 million people. After the independence, many Europeans left Algeria. This culminated in loss of management of farms and factories, extensive areas of abandoned lands and, most importantly, with only 10,000 French teachers remaining in the country.

What can we learn from it? The French colonial rule of Algeria was characterized by a violent approach. Before the war started, there were several peaceful attempts at, if not necessarily advocating for independence, improving the living conditions of Algerians by promoting a more equal treatment. However, all the peaceful attempts were silenced and repressed, reaching its boiling point during the Setif massacre. What we can learn from the Algerian War is that some claims cannot be silenced by violence. More than mere independence from colonial rule, the right of self-determination is a longing that will thrive despite violence and repression of any kind.

The Second Sudanese Civil War (1983-2005)

What happened? Since its independence in 1956, Sudan has lived more days at war than it has at peace. Divided by the southern Sudanese non-Arab population and northern Sudanese Arab population, Sudan's ethnic and religious tensions seemed to be finally contained after the signing of the *Addis Ababa Agreement* in 1972, which ended the First Sudanese Civil War. The agreement conceded southern Sudan the right to self-determination, particularly regarding religion, as well as the autonomy on internal matters, making it the Southern Sudan Autonomous Region. However, in 1978, oil fields were discovered on the border between north and south Sudan. The economic profit of the oil fields incited new conflicts, however, the Second Sudanese Civil War would not begin until 1983.

In an attempt to Islamize Sudan, President Jaafar Nimeiry and his military regime, violated the 1972's agreement by imposing Sharia Law, terminating southern autonomy. Considering most constitutionally-guaranteed rights were suspended, the non-Arab population was subject to Sharia's trials and punishments. The southern response came from the Sudanese People's Liberation Movement (SPLM) under the leadership of John Garang.

The civil war lasted for twenty years and included several attempts to cease fire, and high amounts of international assistance (the supply of weapons as well as elements of humanitarian aid such as medicine, food and water) and international action (including economic sanctions, the harshest being the US's after the discovery of Osama bin Laden was sheltering in Sudan, denouncement of human rights violations and attempts of establishing an agreement).

The war finally came to an end with the Comprehensive Peace Agreement of 2005, leaving a total of 2.5 million dead and 4 million displaced.

The Comprehensive Peace Agreement of 2005: After twenty years of a violent civil war, causing millions of deaths and displacements, negotiations to bring an end to it began. Finally, in January 2005 the Comprehensive Peace Agreement (CPA) was signed, providing Sudanese people with the long hoped for ceasefire. The agreement contained the following terms: southern Sudan autonomy would be restored for six years and, in 2011, a referendum would be held to decide on the secession; the income from the oilfields, which represented 73% of Sudan's export revenues, would be shared in half by north and south Sudan; Islamic law would remain only in the north. A power-sharing government was also established, with John Garang as a vice-president. With the death of Garang, Salva Kiir Mayardiit succeeded him.

Darfur: Although the Civil War officially came to an end in 2005, the Darfur region had been the stage of ethnic violence since 2003, which continued despite the alleged ceasefire. The conflict in the region started after an uprising of two rebel groups regarding unjust treatment of the non-Arab population based on religious intolerance. The government responded with a genocidal campaign against the non-Arab population of the region, despite the fact that they were supposedly pushing forward the peace agreement. The campaign resulted in 400 thousand Darfuris killed as a result of the ethnic cleansing, as well as more than 3 million displaced. President Omal al-Bashir, who had been in power since 1989 (and who was later overthrown by a coup d'état in 2019), made Darfuris survivors' lives harder by making more difficult the access to emergency aid supply of food and medicine. Al-Bashir was indicted by the International Criminal Court (ICC) for crimes against humanity, war crimes and genocide.

New state born: In January 2011, after the established six years by the Comprehensive Peace Agreement, southern Sudanese voted on a referendum on secession. The result was in favor of full independence from Sudan. On July 9, known as Independence Day, South Sudan emerged as a new state, with autonomy and sovereignty. Yet, the civil war continued to be a part of South Sudan's history, due to a dispute between President Salva Kiir Mayardit and Vice-President Riek Machar in 2012. The conflict comes to an end in 2018 with a power-sharing agreement and, posteriorly in 2020, the creation of a transitional government of national unity. Today, however, South Sudan remains ravaged by the consequences of continuous years of civil war: it is one of the world's poorest countries, with nearly 82% of the population living in extreme poverty, high mortality rate and low life expectancy. South Sudan is still permeated by violence and human rights violations in the present day.

What can we learn from it? Resulting in a humanitarian crisis that has lasted until now, the Second Sudanese Civil War had no victor, only a clear message of failure of the human race as a whole. Motivated by a dispute over the control of oil fields and religious prejudice, the conflict had serious consequences that will continue to be seen for years to come. Amidst the genocide and displacement of millions (creating a new refugee crisis), humanitarian crisis of all kinds, Sudanese people have gone through the unthinkable and the unbearable. Killing was indiscriminate, with both sides of the war being equally violent and indifferent towards human rights and, even, human life.

Today, after the independence of South Sudan, both Sudan and South Sudan still suffer from war fallouts, with what is called a "lost generation" due to the lack of investment and, consequently, the absence of educational opportunities, access to basic health care, and employment opportunities.

The main lesson we can learn from the Second Sudanese Civil War is that the guaranteeing and protection of human rights must be a priority for sovereign states and the international community. Even though international interference, either through neighboring states welcoming and sheltering refugees or international organizations intervening in order to protect and assist those in deplorable life conditions, was present throughout the conflict and the present day, more could have been done. In a situation where there is a complete disregard and even violation of human rights on the government's behalf, it is the international community's duty and the human rights international law system to intervene despite states' sovereignty.

The Angolan Civil War (1975-2002)

Independence and nationalist movements: The Portuguese colonial rule of Angola was outlined by forced labor upon locals. This, in conjunction with land expropriation, was the ignition to rebellions as early as 1961. The Portuguese government replied through the deployment of troops.

There were three main nationalist liberation groups that would later fight among themselves during the twenty-year-long civil war that ravaged the country. Firstly, the Popular Movement for the Liberation of Angola (Movimento Popular de Libertação de Angola; MPLA) was founded in 1956 and as of 1962 it was led by Agostinho Neto. Secondly, the National Liberation Front of Angola (Frente Nacional de Libertação de Angola; FNLA) advocated for the restoration and defense of the Kongo empire, founded in 1962. And, thirdly, the National Union for the Total Independence of Angola (União Nacional para a Independência Total de Angola; UNITA) was founded in 1966 by Jonas Savimbi. Thus, Angola's lack of a unified independence movement was quickly followed by a civil war between the three nationalist fronts.

The independence was officially achieved on November 11, 1975, after the Portuguese Prime Minister Marcello Caetano was overthrown in April 1974. After a bloody war in Portugal that resulted in the coup of Caetano, the Portuguese army was deeply overworked and simply left Angola without any effort to impose peace or supervise elections. Consequently, it was the MPLA that seized control of the capital city, declared itself the government of newly independent Angola and was validated by several African countries. Due to the

MPLA's reluctance to share power with its counterparts, the FNLA and the UNITA, created a rival government in order to implement their own national plan. These two groups also sought the aid of South African forces. Thus, the civil war began in 1975, when the UNITA formally declared war on the MPLA.

The Angolan Civil War: The MPLA was supported by the Ambundu people, Angola's second-largest ethnic group, while the UNITA and the FNLA were backed by the Ovimbundu people and the Bakongo people, respectively. The MPLA was unable to influence rural areas because for one, they ruled from the capital and, second, it was a movement composed by an urban class. Therefore, the rural areas were dominated by FNLA and UNITA.

South African forces invaded Angola, siding with both the FNLA and the UNITA. As a response, Cuban troops sided with the MPLA. Considering all these groups there were nearly 50,000 soldiers stationed in Angola. The Cuban forces were able to push South Africans out of Angola and gain control of all the provincial capitals. The FNLA went into exile where it grew weaker, leaving the confrontation almost entirely between the MPLA and UNITA.

In 1977, the MPLA transformed itself into a Marxist-Leninist party adding 'Labor Party' (Partido Trabalhista) to its name, and seeking the implementation of economic communism. This caught international attention due to the fact that the period was characterized by an upsurge of Cold War's tensions, thus, the civil war became a Cold War proxy.

Funding and the Cold War: Angola is one of the countries that is richest in resources, so that in the beginning of the war, groups took advantage of them to fund their enterprise. The MPLA controlled Luanda and the coastal region, where much of the oil was concentrated, thus, using the coastal oil revenue as funding for its rule. The UNITA, dominated the geographic region where most diamond reserves were located and benefited from this wealth to sustain its rebellion. The MPLA received immense amounts of aid from the Soviet Bloc, including financial and military support from the Soviet Union and the military intervention from Cuba. It is worth noting, however, that the war would only begin to be considered as a Cold War proxy in 1985, when the UNITA started receiving US support. The UNITA was backed by the US economically and militarily, encouraging South Africa to give its technical and tactical support as well, aiming to rebuild UNITA's military capacity. UNITA's attacks became increasingly effective, particularly when considering their strategy of targeting oil installations (MPLA's funding source). In turn, MPLA was forced to adopt a more conciliatory approach.

Conclusion: In 1989, after the disruption of South Africa's support to the UNITA and the withdrawal of the Cuban troops, negotiations started between Savimbi, UNITA's leader, and dos Santos, MPLA's leader after Neto's death. The negotiations, aimed at a ceasefire agreement, were unfruitful. Coinciding with the international breakdown of communism, chiefly the dissolution of the Soviet Union, the MPLA started to distance itself from the Marxist-Leninist approach, abandoning the 'PT' from its name. The MPLA also renounced the one-party state by producing a new constitution that included elections and participation by all.

Elections were held in 1992, under the supervision of the United Nations. Dos Santos was elected president in what was understood by the UNITA as a fraudulent election leading to the rekindling of the civil war. Moreover, after the election, UNITA's delegates were murdered in Luanda, it is believed this was owed to the government's backing. This once again provoked the suspension of the truce negotiations. This time, however, the government, represented by the MPLA, gained support abroad, including from former opponents: South Africa and the United States. The UN imposed sanctions against the UNITA for violating a previously accepted ceasefire, and the international pressure to start negotiations with the MPLA continued to rise.

In November 1994, the *Lusaka Accord* was signed by both parties, determining UNITA would ceasefire and be incorporated into the government. Although the agreement was signed by both factions, there was reluctance on the UNITA's side, voiced by its leader, Savimbi, who in 1997 refused to attend the ceremony of the UNITA delegates officially joining the government. Besides that, minor fighting between the two groups continued. The tensions exacerbated once more with the civil war in the Democratic Republic of the Congo. Whilst the MPLA government supported the rebel faction led by Laurent Kabila, UNITA instead supported the Zairean regime. UNITA's delegates were then expelled from the government.

Peace was only attained until 2002, after the assassination of UNITA's obstinate leader Savimbi. The peace agreement was signed in April 2002, bringing the twenty-year-long conflict to a close. After the war, it was imperative to rebuild Angola's physical and social infrastructure. Owing to the poor sanitary conditions, the country faced repeated outbreaks of illness. In relation to agricultural production, Angola had thousands of land mines spread throughout the country. Not to mention the human casualties and displacement of 4 million people.

What can we learn from it? The conflict between the three nationalist groups that culminated in the Angolan Civil War was deeply motivated by each party wanting to implement its project for the newborn nation. In the process, the country was ravaged by twenty-seven-years of bombings, assassinations and widespread destruction.

The main lesson we can learn from the Angolan Civil War is that the end does not justify the means. The UNITA resorted to violence and guerrilla warfare in order to overthrow the MPLA government, take power and finally implement its project for the nation. In the process of doing so, the country was severely destroyed, generating long-lasting consequences, including the inability to implement any of the projects. Sometimes the final objective can be forgotten, leading to sabotage by the same people that dreamt and advocated for it.

Boko Haram in Nigeria (2002-Present)

Boko Haram: Boko Haram is an Islamic sectarian movement founded in 2002 by Muslim cleric Mohammed Yusuf in north-eastern Nigeria. The name 'Boko Haram', meaning "Westernization is Sacrilege", was attributed to the group by outsiders, who recognized the group's striking characteristic of antipathy towards the Western civilization. Initially, the movement's intended to wipe out corruption and injustice (phenomena that were believed to be inherited from the West), and to impose Sharia (Islamic law).

The group's trajectory can be divided in two phases. The first phase is marked by their withdrawal from society, with the establishment of camps and schools in the regions of Borno and Yobe. Due to police pressure and presence this was a rather quiet phase of Boko Haram that lasted until 2005. The movement initiated operations against the police, reaching direct confrontation with the Nigerian police and even the military. In 2009, Nigeria's military responded through the Joint Military Task Force operation, assaulting Mohammed Yusuf's compound and associated mosques. This procedure culminated in the death of more than 700 Boko Haram members and the destruction of the mosque/headquarter of the group. Yusuf and other leaders were arrested, however, they were victims of extrajudicial killings by the police and their bodies were displayed in public.

This event enraged the group unleashing Boko Haram's second phase, a much more violent one. Quiet and off the radar for a while after the incident, it was believed that Boko Haram was obsolete. In September 2010, nonetheless, Boko Haram carried out a prison break, releasing nearly 700 prisoners, including 100 members of the group. Since 2010, the group has taken part in a series of attacks, which have increased in frequency and magnitude (including targeted assassinations) focusing on: the military, the police, teachers, universities, banks, markets, Christian preachers and churches. Boko Haram has been able, during its more violent phase, to exert power in the north-eastern section of Nigeria, overthrowing police and army control, and disseminating terror in Nigeria and the neighboring countries. It is believed that this has been enabled by the connections with other terrorist groups.

Regional response: Although the Nigerian government's overall response has been to repress violence with violence, there have been attempts at dialogue. During a media interview in 2011, President Goodluck Jonathan invited Boko Haram to open a dialogue with the government, however, the group responded by confirming its intent to continue fighting. Later on, in 2013, the Nigerian President offered to grant amnesty to the group's militants if they disarmed in an attempt to open communication once more. The proposal was denied by the group and coordinated attacks were launched soon after. Afterwards, in an effort to facilitate the legal prosecution of its members, the President officially declared Boko Haram a terrorist group, banning it under Nigerian law.

Casting these episodes aside, the government's strategy has been predominantly to combat violence with violence. Since then there have been states of emergency declared, curfews, joint task forces, and borders with neighboring countries being closed, but Boko Haram continues to attack with violence. Hence, there is widespread violence on both sides of the conflict: Boko Haram's attacks are constantly evolving (more recently, they started using suicide bombers), and in the government's responses, they kill indiscriminately alleged Boko Haram members and many others as a casualty. The most affected groups are civilians, who are being killed by both.

International response: Boko Haram has been in action in Nigeria since 2010, yet, the international community turned its attention to the group only in 2014. In that year, the group's killing of civilians increased, targeting especially schools and including shocking episodes such as the kidnapping of more than 275 girls from a school in Chibok, the assassination of fifty male students and the destruction of their college in Yobe. The international response was of condemnation and offerings of international assistance. However, the Nigerian government has not taken advantage of the offers. The United Nations imposed sanctions on individuals in Boko Haram, including the freeze of assets, travel bans and arms embargoes. Beyond this, the international response has been minimal, greatly due to the accusations of severe human rights violations perpetrated by Nigerian security forces.

What can we learn from it? As technology and society evolve, the traditional form of war becomes obsolete. Ergo, as new forms of war and conflicts emerge, sometimes we do not yet know how to handle them. Boko Haram is the perfect example of this new type of war, perpetrated by an informal group, in attacks that indiscriminately kill civilians and government officials. The enemy, this time, is not as easy to spot, he takes the disguise of a 'normal' civilian, hiding in plain sight.

The history of Boko Haram in Nigeria and its attacks can teach us that there are new threats in the modern world. Threats that we might not quite understand yet: their purpose is not clear to us, the way they organize is unusual, and the militants look just like an ordinary person.

The lesson we can take from this is that the world is constantly changing, and so are the threats and dangers. However, violence does not seem to be a solution. As demonstrated by the Nigerian government's response to Boko Haram, violence does not repress or end violence, instead, it is responsible for the number of casualties increasing, for the killing of civilians.

The Arab Spring in North Africa (2010-2011)

What happened? In December 2010, Mohamed Bouazizi, a twenty-six-year-old Tunisian street vendor, self-immolated outside a government office after a police attempt to shut down his business. The action encouraged Tunisian protesters and, with the help of social media, the protests were documented and shared online, in turn, inspiring other anti-government demonstrations.

The protests spread from Tunisia to Egypt, Libya and, to a certain extent, to Morocco and Sudan. Although these anti-government uprisings have different particularities, they all share their main catalysts: years of accumulated tensions, challenges and repression exerted by long-standing authoritarian regimes. The outcome, however, was different on every country.

Tunisia, the point of origin of the Arab Spring, is considered successful since it reached lasting democratic progress after President Zine al-Abidine Ben Ali stepped down, and a free election took place.

Despite its initial and partial success, Egypt backslid. After the removal of President Hosni Mubarak, the military seized power and prioritized stability instead of democratic blossom.

Libya's protests escalated into a civil war in 2014 in which rebel forces gained control of Benghazi and created unrest in Tripoli. This was followed by the creation of a rebel leadership council, the Transitional National Council (TNC).

What motivated the Arab uprisings? There are a few similarities worth pointing out regarding the causes that led up to the domestic tension in all the countries that experienced Arab Spring's protests. The countries in question—Tunisia, Egypt, and Libya—were liberalized autocracies, meaning that even though liberal democracy was not a reality, partial liberalization did exist with some degree of tolerance for political dissonance and other political parties. Nonetheless, the process of governance completely excluded active popular participation and political expression was repressed. There were also several reports of human rights violations, as well as a denial of basic civil rights. Additionally, the economy likewise played a role in galvanizing the Arab Spring. Alongside a global price spiking in food and energy in late 2010, social unrest commenced, driven by the rising unemployment and the decrease of living standard. This was accompanied by a general disapproval of the ever present corruption in the governments. Thus, political discontentment with the long-dated autocracies and economic deprivation motivated the movements that became known as the Arab Spring, demanding democratic rule, basic human rights and better life conditions.

Tunisia: Known as the Jasmine Revolution, the popular uprising in Tunisia that inspired similar protests throughout North Africa, started with Mohamed Bouazizi setting himself on fire outside a government building in Sidi Bouzid. This served as a political act that represented the popular discontent with the injustice of the then liberalized autocracy of President Zine al-Abidine Ben Ali, and the economic difficulties felt all around the country. Social uprisings took over the country, protesting unemployment, poverty and political repression. The protests quickly escalated into a denouncement of Ben Ali's 23 year-long regime, accompanied by demands for his removal from power. In a desperate attempt to restore order, the president announced a series of economic and political reforms that did not manage to convince the protesters. Moreover, the regime excluded the Tunisian army from any political role, inducing their refusal to control rioters and the consequent collapse of the regime. Ben Ali fled to Saudi Arabia and his party, the Rassemblement Constitutionnelle Démocratique (RCD) was officially dissolved by the Tunisian court.

Egypt: The Tahrir Revolution, as it became known, represents the social uprisings in Egypt of the notorious Arab Spring. Motivated by Tunisia, opposition parties made up of youths took to the streets in an attempt to overthrow Hosni Mubãrak, thirty year-long president of Egypt. On January 25, 2011, at Tahrir Square in Cairo, the first coordinated mass protest occurred. Successfully resisting police, the demonstrations continued to spread around the country, with the participation of millions of Egyptians demanding free elections and democracy. Mubarak's resilient regime repressed protesters with increased violence, resulting in the death of hundreds. As a last resource, Mubarak announced partial concessions to ease the public—the promise of stepping down after the end of his term in 2011 and the nomination of Omar Suleiman as his first vice-president—which proved ineffective when faced with the public demand for democracy. Finally, after nearly three weeks of protest and social unrest, Mubarak stepped down, and the military took control over the country. With the responsibility to rebuild the state in a more democratic way, the military formed an alliance with the Muslim Brotherhood, added minimalist amendments to the constitution while more significant changes were cast aside.

Libya: With transformations in Tunisia and Egypt brought by social uprisings, expectations for change in Libya grew more each day. The demonstrations initiated after the arrest of a human rights lawyer on February 15, 2011. Protesters faced water cannons and rubber bullets used by the Libyan security forces, however, interestingly enough, a detachment of the Libyan army in Benghazi supported the demonstrators. The situation escalated when, in an attempt to suppress the upheavals, Colonel Muammar Qaddafi, an authoritarian dictator, resorted to lethal force: firing live ammunition, attacking with tanks and artillery on the ground and, from the air, with warplanes and helicopter gunships. The government also restricted communications, including the internet. What began as social demonstrations of discontentment with the regime became an armed rebellion and, quickly, the country was consumed by a violent civil war. The country became, thus, divided in half, with Benghazi under the control of the rebel forces and Tripoli still under the domain of the authoritarian regime. Qaddafi was overthrown, tortured and executed in October 2011, leaving the country in a state of civil war.

What is the legacy of the uprisings? The Arab Spring in these three countries of North Africa produced three very different outcomes.

Tunisia made a lasting shift to democracy, and increased internet freedom—an important catalyst in the spread of the Arab Spring—due to the protection of free expression and free press in the 2014 constitution. And, even though women empowerment was not a main target of the protests, there are now more women speaking out and participating more effectively in the government.

Egypt, on the other hand, is considered only partially successful. Despite the fact that the thirty-year-long autocracy was overthrown, Egypt's democracy backslid under the rule of the military, experiencing a downturn in both press and internet freedom. There have been aggressive attempts to suppress press freedom and a subsequent increase in journalist arrests since 2013. In the same fashion, internet control has tightened with the establishment of censoring laws and restricted internet access.

Moreover, Libya saw no democratic improvements whatsoever. The Libyan Civil War, also referred to as the Libyan Crisis, lasted for 9 more years, finally coming to an end in 2020. During these rough years, Libya was ruled by two opposing governments in separate regions of the country, and Libyans faced violence and scarce access to food, resources and healthcare services, resulting in a refugee crisis with thousands escaping to Europe.

What can we learn from it? When the Arab Spring started in Tunisia with the successful falling of the authoritarian regime, hope for the same outcome disseminated throughout other countries. However, as discussed above, the three North African countries —Tunisia, Egypt and Libya—had discrepant results. This teaches us that rebellions, riots and uprisings are not a guarantee of regime transformation and democratic advancement. Creating and, especially, maintaining democracy depends on a series of other factors that, most of the time, are not under civilian's power. Thus, as essential as social uprisings and political action are, regime revolution is not an assurance.

The Western Africa Ebola Virus Epidemic (2014-2016)

What happened? The Ebola virus disease (EVD), also known as Ebola hemorrhagic fever, is an illness responsible for several outbreaks in the Western African countries between 2014 and 2016.

Whereas it was discovered as early as 1976, it was not until the virus' outbreaks in 2014-2016 that epidemic proportions were reached. The first known patient was reported in December 2013, in Guinea. Guinea's outbreak rapidly spread to its capital and neighboring countries, Liberia and Sierra Leone, making them the three most contaminated countries. Only in August 2014 would the World Health Organization (WHO) declare the Western African situation to be a Public Health Emergency of International Concern (PHEIC), which meant that the outbreak would then be understood as representing a risk of international spread and/or require a coordinated international response.

At first, the virus circulated in urban areas, in counterpoint to earlier cases of the disease which were mainly concentrated in rural areas. Correspondingly, the virus' transmission speed increased, reaching other African countries such as Mali, Nigeria, Senegal, and even countries in other continents, like Italy, Spain, United Kingdom and the United States. While some countries handled the health crisis promptly and efficiently, others struggled with deficient health care systems and infrastructure problems. Liberia, Sierra Leone and Guinea, the epicenter of the epidemic, finally declared themselves Ebola-free in 2016. The outbreak left 11,325 dead and around 28,600 cases.

Liberia's case. Liberia was the country with the largest number of cases, which deeply affected the country's socioeconomic development.

The response came from local leaders, which focused their efforts on promoting behaviors such as hygiene and other effective habits in the prevention of the virus. One important practice changed respected funeral rites: it was part of the custom to wash deceased bodies before burial, which represented great danger in terms of infection. Furthermore, clinical care and public health responses also had an important part in managing the crisis. Liberia was declared Ebola-free on two occasions in 2015 that followed the discovery of new cases in two occasions during May and September. On June 1, 2016, the final announcement was made. Liberia's deficient health care system was competent enough to counteract the epidemic, although many lives were lost in the process. The international response, interestingly enough, only arrived after the epidemic had already been dealt with.

Nigeria's response. The Nigerian response to the Ebola virus outbreak is considered exemplary. The first case of EVD in Nigeria was confirmed on the July 25, 2014, followed by a prompt reaction from the government with the mobilization of the Federal Ministry of Health (FMOH), the Nigerian Center for Disease Control (NCDC) and the Nigeria Field Epidemiology and Laboratory Training Program (NFELTP). Although the virus was able to spread to Lagos and Port Harcourt, Nigeria contested the originally predicted number of cases and deaths, thought to increase at a catastrophic rate. The above-mentioned institutions were fundamental in the handling of the outbreak: in a coordinated response, they monitored and tracked suspected cases in order to slow down the contagion. Apart from that, the Port Health services monitored all national entry points, by land, sea and air, examining both the people entering and leaving the country. This coordinated response from government institutions helped contain the virus and prevent its spread to other neighboring virus-free cities and countries.

That being said, the Nigerian health system was not prepared whatsoever for the epidemic, causing the redirection of funds destined for other health system activities to managing the Ebola epidemic. As a consequence, one measure that was pivotal in lessening the epidemic's impact on the country was an awareness campaign. Since EVD is a disease transmitted mostly by contact with infected bodily fluids, the best prevention is personal healthcare. In such a manner, the awareness campaign emphasized the importance of handwashing and other hygiene measures as well as information about signs and symptoms.

Impact. The Ebola virus epidemic was declared finished in March 2016, after the Public Health Emergency of International Concern (PHEIC) status was lifted by the WHO. Western African countries had held this classification since the beginning of the epidemic. The final death toll consisted of 28,000 cases and 11,000 deaths in West Africa, as well as a severely affected healthcare system in the region.

The healthcare workforce was the most acutely affected by the epidemic, Liberia, for instance, lost 8% of its doctors and nurses to EVD. Alongside that, due to the countries' unpreparedness to handle an epidemic, resources had to be redirected resulting in a shortage of healthcare inputs and aggravating the situation of other diseases by delaying treatments and controls, such as HIV, tuberculosis, measles and malaria.

The epidemic also had economic impact, costing a total of $4.3 billion USD and a decline in trade as governments feared risk of infection and outbreaks in their countries. The social impact, in turn, is immeasurable.

What can we learn from it? Viruses and diseases have been around since the beginning of mankind and are certainly not going to cease to exist. In this sense, the next epidemic (if not a pandemic) is not a question of if, but a question of when. As exemplified by the Western African countries when faced with the Ebola outbreak, most countries are not prepared to manage an epidemic. Investment in a functioning and effective healthcare system should be a government priority, in order to prevent casualties. Besides that, when it comes to matters regarding public and global health, governments should not be the only ones involved in handling it. Elements that concern humankind as a whole such as epidemics and pandemics should be resolved with a juxtaposed response between international organizations and sovereign countries. Cooperation is key in lessening the health, humanitarian and social consequences of disease outbreaks. Additionally, the episode also enlightens us about the need for quick responses. As demonstrated by the too-late international response to Liberia, actions should be taken quickly. When it comes to health matters, postponement to act can culminate in hundreds to thousands of deaths.

Chapter II: Asia

Benjamin Ian Chen

The Chinese Civil War (1927-1949)

What happened? After the 1911 revolution led by Sun-Yat Sen with his group of revolutionaries, the Qing Dynasty fell, leading to the establishment of the Republic of China (R.O.C). After Sun-Yat Sen passed away in 1925, one of the military leaders, Chang Kai-Shek, took over and decided to remove the warlords, a turmoil that plagued China for years. He successfully executed his expedition and controlled seven provinces in Guangdong. This makes him think that military generals controlling different states are not a menace, incentivizing him to get rid of one of the potential threats to the KMT at the time—the CCP. During this time period, both the Kuomintang (KMT) and newly formed Chinese Communist Party (CCP) were supported by the Communist Soviet Union, causing a power struggle between the two parties. The Chinese Civil War resolved the issue of which party would control China. Although the KMT held higher military capacity, corruption and inflation led to ineffective government structure, costing them the people's support. It ended with the CCP taking over and forcing the KMT party to flee to Taiwan. This Civil War ended with an estimated 9.5 million people killed. We will be looking at why the KMT failed and how the CCP stabilized the Chinese people after such a horrible event and built China into one of the dominating world powers of the modern era.

Why did KMT lose? There are various reasons for this. The main one being the Second Sino-Japanese War, which started in 1937. The fall of the monarchical system resulted in an unstructured government, with different regions of China controlled by different military men seeking power. Chiang Kai-Shek, the KMT leader in this period, dedicated his time to fighting the communist instead of the Japanese, which went against the extremely popular nationalist values of the time. If he had not focused his efforts in fighting the CCP, he might have had a chance to remain in power. However, we should bear in mind that Sun-Yat Sen, Chiang Kai Shek and Mao Tse-Tung had the intention of making

China a better place. That being said, the differences in their approach ushered significant and unnecessary deaths and losses.

Establishing governing power's foundation: In Mao Zedong's "On the People's Democratic Dictatorship", he proposed to first destroy any and all pre-revolutionary organizations and replace them with CCP controlled institutions. On top of that, he established a completely new economic and political order involving control over all parts of CCP's jurisdiction. Later on, the establishment of mutual aid teams, new irrigation systems and installment of CCP associations in rural areas played a crucial role in consolidating Mao's control over the Chinese people.

Land Reformation: In response to the unstable economy after the revolution, the CCP enforced policies that allowed the central government to purchase producers with state controlled market output. Essentially, the market became state-controlled. To add on, the push for elimination of feudalism allowed for the reallocation of all the resources towards building new social institutions and public service that directly increases living standards for the people. This is the redistribution of wealth and power, in other words, the socialism that Mao has been advocating for.

First Five-Year Plan (1953 – 1957): The First Five-Year Plan, known as Wunian Jihua, was focusing its effort in developing a solid foundation for China to industrialize. It is a plan based on Soviet Union's model for economic development through industrialization and agricultural development. The Chinese government utilized "Collectivization", with policies such as having mutual aid teams (MAT). People participating in MAT will need to share labor and resources with each other. Down the line, we had the establishment of Agricultural Producers Cooperatives (APC) which involved 50 households sharing resources together. Finally, Mao gradually progressed with these changes and ended up combining 250 households together, in which people's property would be considered the property of the cooperative. By 1956, 67.5% of industrial enterprises were owned by the state and no privately owned enterprises were left. Overall, The First Five-Year Plan was successful in the sense that it increased the country's economic growth and expanded to different industries, as we see industrial production rate increased by 19% on a yearly basis.

The Second Five-Year Plan; The Great Leap Forward (1958 – 1960): This is a very ironic title, the "Great Leap" was an indicator of Mao's efforts to transform China from socialism to communism in order to surpass the Soviet Union. Collectivization was reaching its final stage, with communes that held up to 5500+ households. Mao thought China could become the leading force in the world in terms of steel production with a 2000% increase in production within five years.

During that time, devotion to Mao's regime was very common, and people were hoping to produce more grains in order to give a better impression. The competition between communes on who could produce more resources steered people to report false amounts of grain produced. As we all know, governments base their tax rate on the economic performance, hence, the production number being so steep led to an increase in tax rate of up to 28%. The state over-taxed the population and often collected the entire production from the communes, causing widespread famine as well as an estimate of 30 million deaths due to starvation.

When reflecting on the causes of famine, it is clear that it is mainly due to natural phenomenon: the weather damaged the production of grains causing little output, making it so people would have to turn over their whole production to the government and starve as a result. As the Association for Asian Studies points out, when famine occurred in the Soviet Union, 6 million people died, while 5% of the total population perished in North Korea back in 1995. They concluded that "the overall fall in famine mortality over the past century is due to *the growth of democracy* across the globe" (Brown 2012, 34).

The Korean War (1950-1953)

What happened? In order to understand this war from its roots it is essential to know that the Japanese Empire collapsed around the end of World War II and left Korea (former colony of Japan) with no support. The two strongest powers in the world —the Soviet Union and the United States— divided Korea into two parts, in accordance with the 38th parallel, North Korea (communist) and South Korea (democratic). Five years later, North Korea launched an attack in order to unify Korea once again. This triggered the sensitive relation between the Soviet Union and the United States. The latter proceeded to call upon the United Nations Security Council troops to be deployed in Korea as a means to curb the spread of communism. Conflicts occurred between the two parties, with the communist North Korea backed by the communists Soviet Union and China, and the democratic South Korea backed by the United States and fellow UN member nations. The combat ended in the same situation on top of 2.5 million killed, and the establishment of the demilitarized zone (DMZ) that separates North Korea and South Korea to this very day. We will also see the Korean War being the spark that gradually led to the Cold War.

What was in it for both sides? For the United States, the Korean War was an example of the democratic country's effort to constrain communism from dispersing. They successfully gained endorsement from the UN and led the efforts in fighting North Korea. Most importantly, if South Korea had not been aided by the US, communism would have taken control of Korea as a whole. Some people argued that the US's foreign intervention should have been limited to offering free migration access for South Koreans to the United States to prevent innocent civilians from getting hurt. This remains the main point of debate among people.

By successfully preventing the North Korean government from taking over the entirety of Korea, the prevalence of the United Nations was also guaranteed. At that moment, the UN had only been established for five years and if North Korea had defied the verdict of its Security Council it "would have meant that the United Nations would have ceased to exist as a serious instrumentality for the maintenance of international peace" (Dudziak 1 Mar. 2019) as per an informal State Department memo. Therefore, the protection of the United Nations can be considered as one of the US's major interests to participate in this war as well.

The Soviet Union, through the loss of millions of lives and the population cutting back on resources to support the North Korean front, succeeded in sparking a conflict by demonstrating their own power and capability. This war can be viewed as the conflict between socialism and capitalism, yet, for South Korea, it set the path towards the democratic government in place today.

South Korea's rebuilding after the war: Syngman Rhee was the first president after the war who utilized an authoritarian government in an attempt to provide stability to the Korean people. Rhee's Liberal Party used bribery and manipulation to retain power. This incited an instant reply from the Korean people who started to demand a better and more democratic government. Rhee's economic policies were not the best either. He established an import substitution industrialization policy that encouraged local industries by blocking imports. Korea's tiny internal market and resources paved the road for the failure of Rhee's economic policy. Rhee also refused to establish economic friendly agreements with Japan, Korea's former enemy, due to the fear that Korea would become Japan's economic "colony".

Throughout that time, the United States constantly provided aid to the South Korean government to the point that it accounted for 80% of Korea's Gross National Product. Later on, Rhee passed

National Security Laws which he leveraged to execute opposition powers. Ultimately, this led to an uprising organized by students that caused Rhee's exile to Hawaii.

In 1950, a constitution was established that guaranteed a parliament that still placed the old regime as the central power. The leader, Park, attempted to devalue the currency leading to inflation and working conditions remaining poor. Once again, a group of army officers overthrew the government in thirteen months. In general terms, under Rhee's and Park's administration, the economy was still keeping Korean people in extreme poverty.

The Vietnam War (1955-1975)

What happened? The Vietnam War was the conflict between North Vietnam against South Vietnam. The United States backed South Vietnam in order to curb the expansion of communism. Meanwhile, communist countries like China and Russia supported North Vietnam. This war can also be referred to as a manifestation of the Cold War between the United States and Russia.

The reason behind the conflict between South & North Vietnam is the desire for Vietnam to unify the entire country under a communist government in accordance with models provided by countries like China. South Vietnam on the other hand was extremely Westernized and wished to be close allies with the United States. The United States stationed 500,000 military personnel in Vietnam, while China and Russia provided technology and resources for North Vietnam. By 1973, the United States withdrew its troops and South Vietnam collapsed. Finally, the war ended with the death of 2 million civilians, 250,000 South Vietnam soldiers and 58,200 American soldiers.

We will be reviewing policies that were used to make up for the damages caused by the War considering Vietnam's industries were disrupted, and their infrastructures destroyed; agricultural land in central Vietnam was poisoned by chemical agents and scattered with land mines, resulting in the limitation of agricultural production as there was less land available. Vietnam heavily relied on the foreign aid provided by Russia and China to keep its economy running during the war. The sudden withdrawal of the aid soon revealed Vietnam's true economy—unstable and fragile. During these difficult times, the Socialist Republic of Vietnam was formed.

Establishing the government: The Communist Party of Vietnam (CPV) needed to deal with the separation of its people in order to lay the ground for political decisions. The South Vietnam leaders fled to other countries, but millions of their supporters were extremely anti-communism. The government established re-education camps in order to neutralize threats of potential opponents, including the South Vietnamese Army's related soldiers and officers, who endured poor living conditions. There were more than 120,000 people in the camps all the way until the 1990s.

Economic policies from the CPV: First, the government eradicated all private entities and established state owned enterprises. This allowed more direct control from the government. Second, the Land Reformation. The government redistributed lands for better utilization, prohibiting landlords from ripping off peasants. This policy played out differently in different regions of Vietnam. On one hand, North Vietnam's economic situation was relatively worse considering people owned nothing. On the other hand, peasants in South Vietnam owned extended areas of land due to reformation projects implemented by the United States. It is important to remember that the Land Reformation was often perceived by the people as collectivization, which was proven to cause mass famine in China. Based on these reasons, the Land Reformation policy took longer than it should have, reaching only a partial coverage of Vietnam.

The Vietnam War left 58 million people in Vietnam in need of food. The government attempted to increase production of crops and in return offered an adequate amount of food to each citizen. Notwithstanding, the production goals were not achieved, causing starvation and governmental dissatisfaction among citizens, as well as acts of resistance and rebellion across the country. This situation continued all the way to 1979 when the food rationing system was relatively established. In the mid 1980s, the Vietnam government looked to China for more moderate capitalist systems that allowed for small businesses to operate. The reformation was named Doi Moi, which means 'the renovation'.

Foreign participation of Vietnam: In 1977, Vietnam was officially admitted to the United Nations. Later on, the government withdrew troops from Cambodia which led to peace with most of the countries. Foreign aid started pouring in along with acceptance to the IMF and the ASEAN. There were generally no more embargoes or sanctions on Vietnam.

The United States' Role: In order to maintain America's credibility as the freedom defender within the region and to hinder the proliferation of communism, the United States felt compelled to enter the War.

The first military placement in Vietnam from the United States was in 1961. President Kennedy was hoping that US military presence could effectively target what military aid could not accomplish—a fast ending to the war. With no effective results, the subsequent president, President Johnson approved bombing raids in North Vietnam. The South Vietnam government was gradually falling apart when President Johnson ordered even more troops: around 300,000 American soldiers. This led to protests in the United States, as the number of American casualties in Vietnam spiked with no clear signs of the United States winning the war. President Nixon ordered the policy called "Vietnamization" to end US involvement in the Vietnam War, including the withdrawal of American troops and the increased support for South Vietnam soldiers training. Yet, Nixon continued to bomb North Vietnam.

In 1973, a treaty was signed in Paris to end complete US military involvement in order for the North Vietnam government to release all captured American troops. This treaty also provided the grounds for South and North Vietnam to unify relatively "peacefully", although the North Vietnam government killed over 80,000 South Vietnam soldiers after the treaty was signed.

Japan's Lost Decade (1991-2001)

What happened? Ever since 1980, Japan has started to remove restrictions on finance and emphasize the flexibility of capital transactions. Adding on to that, the 1985 *Plaza Accord* spiked the yen (Japanese currency) to its highest point. In order to support the export industry, the Bank of Japan took on an extremely lenient economic policy regarding the currency system, stocks, and assets. These were heavily invested in and increased. However, the Bank of Japan failed to produce emergency plans for the expansion of asset price bubbles. After the asset price bubble burst, Japan's asset prices collapsed rapidly and banks' non-performing debts rose sharply. Manufacturers actively deleverage, bringing not only a "balance sheet recession", but also pushing Japan into a serious "deflationary cycle" (Yamamoto, Chino and Matsumoto 2010, 19).

The Japanese government enforced some effective measures as well as ineffective ones, such as lowering interest rates and an expansionary fiscal policy. It was not until 2005 that Japan's economy started to slowly recover with the international economic situation improving and extreme measures such as quantitative easing policy.

Effects of the lost decade: Firstly, after the bubble burst, asset prices collapsed and assets such as stocks and real estate shrunk sharply. During these ten years, the combined loss in the stocks and real estate dropped by 1500 trillion yen (three years of Japan's GDP!), similar to the 1929's Great Depression.

Secondly, the bank's distressed debt rose sharply. Due to the fact that most banks in Japan held large amounts of stocks as part of their asset portfolio, the asset price collapse forced banks to go out of business. With banks being at potential risk of closing, people started to withdraw their deposits, causing a large-scale bank run within the country. In response to that, the Japanese government provided full protection for people's bank accounts, successfully solving this short term financial crisis.

Thirdly, the bubble caused serious assets and liabilities for enterprises. In order to alleviate their burden, they allocated all their resources in repaying their debts while decreasing their investment and consumption. As a result, we see a significant shift in terms of private demand becoming weaker. Even the "zero interest rate policy" did not incentivize more investment.

Finally, due to a lack of demand in the market, ever since 1998 Japan's core consumer price index (the index to measure macroeconomics and price level) went negative while the deflation rate increased. This leads to an increase in the actual interest rate that further incentivizes spending, we can refer to this situation as a deflationary spiral with no ending.

Policies from the Japanese government: Firstly, the Bank of Japan lowered the rediscount rate all the way from 6% to 0.5%. In 1999, it furthered its plan and went along with a zero interest rate policy in order to decrease the Interbank Offered Rate (the rate at which banks borrow from each other), making money accessible. Between 2001 and 2006, the Bank of Japan enforced a quantitative easing policy in which they purchased long term securities and ABS to stimulate money supply within the economy.

Secondly, as mentioned before the government utilized temporary full protection for deposits in order to prevent bank runs. Plus, the government set up a finance rebuild program with a budget of 60 trillion yen, with measures such as purchasing financial enterprise's preferred stock, and non-performing assets in order to enhance the capital structure of financial institutions. This provided funds to set up transitional banks, implementing special public measures.

Thirdly, in response to low demand in the market, the government spent 134 trillion yen on over eleven economic stimulation programs like reducing tax and increasing financing in public investments.

What can we learn from it? When asset bubbles are gradually increasing, it is essential that the government remembers that this irrational exuberance will not continue indefinitely. The trade-off is something that can be easily overlooked, so we should be utilizing specific policies that target the bubble. Back in the 1980s, the Japanese government failed to respond to the extreme increase in capital price. Later on, they pulled out before their economy could fully recover, which laid the foundation for the Lost Decade. We can look at other countries' response to the 2008 financial crisis and see what they learned from Japan. They learned to evaluate when they should be pulling out after the economy recovers to a certain extent.

In terms of currency policy, the national banks shall be establishing clear conditions as to when the government will be pulling out so that the market can prepare itself.

The Asian Financial Crisis (1997-1998)

What happened? Back in 1997, the Thai government announced that it would no longer peg their currency to the US dollar, adopting instead a floating exchange rate. This induced a more than 60% devaluation of the baht (Thai currency) compared to the dollar, causing a currency crisis within the region, with "tiger economies" crashing down one by one during that time.

Why did the Thai government detach the baht from the dollar?
Ever since the 90s, the massive volume of capital inflow from foreign firms resulted in an annual growth of over 8% in Thailand. Later on, the Thai government proceeded with financial market deregulation and liberalization of capital accounts, the exchange rate remained extremely stable and fixed to the US dollar.

All these accommodating economic policies led to the rapid growth in capital inflow. The situation was so effective that the property sector grew by 395% within six years. However, it is important to see how these foreign capital inflows evolved. Thailand's financial institutions issued too many loans directed to sectors like real-estate which do not build up capital goods. In addition, the safety net provided by the government made banks relaxed about bank runs, resulting in over 50+ banks forced to close down. Thailand had a relatively slower export surge that stunned economic growth, these factors led to the depreciation of the baht. Ever since 1995, economic growth has been stagnant without an effective economical basis, with foreign firms pulling out because there is no profit to remain in Thailand anymore.

Under the fixed exchange rate system, the Thai government used more than 90% of their foreign reserve to maintain the value of the baht, and so there was an inevitable enforcement of a flexible exchange rate system.

On July 2, 1997, Thailand officially adopted a flexible exchange rate system and the Asian Financial Crisis began.

Russia: We will be looking into Russia's response to the financial crisis. As we mentioned before, the Asian Financial Crisis accompanied by the decrease in oil demand directly attacked Russia's foreign exchange reserves. In response to that, the Russian government devalued the ruble (their currency), defaulted on domestic debt and delayed payment on foreign debt. Under the status quo, the Central Bank of the Russian Federation chose to abide with flexible rates with rubles. As a result, inflation rate spiked up to 84% and the government largely decreased subsidies for different sectors, leading to closing or acquisitions between banks.

How did Russia bounce back from this major loss? Between 1999 and 2000, international oil prices spiked up, pushing Russia's oil trading business. Large capital flow that encouraged consumer demand went into Russia, resulting later on in a potential financial crisis.

Singapore: Despite having a strong economic foundation, Singapore was still severely damaged by these uncertain fluctuations. The GDP growth of Singapore went from 8% in 1997 to 1.5% in 1998. Overall, company closures and mass reduction in terms of scale led to a low demand market, with an unemployment rate of 3.2%. In terms of exportation, Asian countries are Singapore's main export location, thus the financial crisis hit Singapore very hard in this respect as well. Weaker demand for oil domestic exports slowed down every aspect of Singapore's economy.

How did the Singapore government respond to the crisis? There are mainly two approaches: 1) Decreasing business costs to incentivize operations; 2) Distributing relief plans towards citizens. The government provided a 15% property tax rebate for businesses and 5% personal income tax rebate. In response to the worsening regional condition, a 2 billion package was distributed with 40% tax rebate for specific areas such as commercial and industrial properties. In less than a year, the Singapore economy gradually got back into shape. The strong manufacturing sector along with regular trading activities successfully pulled Singapore's GDP growth back to around 7%.

How did the international community respond? First and foremost, we can look at the International Monetary Fund's (IMF) response. They provided short term loans worth $110 billion to countries with unstable economies during that time, such as Thailand and South Korea. In exchange, the IMF imposed strict conditions including high taxation and interest rate, decreasing public spending and state-owned firms. After the crisis, economic slowdown was clear to many people who were reluctant to invest in developing areas, leading to a decrease in capital inflow. The situation also led to the fluctuation of the oil's price and fostered oil companies to merge in order to survive by going against the oil price volatility. Most importantly, in response to this crisis and as a defense mechanism against these economic impacts, countries invested in foreign exchange reserves, in which US Treasury Bonds were exclusively purchased by governments.

The Saffron Revolution (2007-2008)

What happened? Stagnant economic growth in Myanmar has always been a contributing factor towards the reason people are protesting against the Myanmar government. Myanmar is listed as one of the poorest countries in the world by the United Nations, along with having the lowest government spending on basic healthcare and educational infrastructures. Additionally, Myanmar's military dictatorship and state terrorism pushed for the public's desire for true democracy and an end to military involvement in politics.

Concretely, what triggered the Saffron Revolution was the decision made by The State Peace and Development Council (SPDC) to remove subsidies for fuels on August 15, 2007. This caused the price to increase by more than 100%. For public transportations, which uses compressed natural gas, the price spiked to 500% in a few days. The protest was dubbed the "Saffron Revolution" after Buddhist monks, who made up a significant amount of the protestors, are widely associated with saffron-colored robes.

The Revolution is reported by UNHRC's Special Reporter Paulo Sergio Pinhero to result in more than 110 killed, 200 injured and 2100 arrested.

The Saffron Revolution is considered a milestone in Myanmar's road to democracy since the failed uprising for democracy in 1988.

This Revolution indirectly led to the establishment of Myanmar's 2015 first non-military government in 54 years.

Why is Myanmar in its current status quo? To understand the situation, we must learn first about Myanmar's government. The leading government of Myanmar is the military junta, which allocates most of its money to the military. Myanmar's economy depends on natural resources, the poverty level is around 26%, this figure is often doubled in rural areas where more than 70% of the total population lives. Myanmar's lack of adequate supply chain and appropriate infrastructure is highly vulnerable to natural hazard, which especially exposes the vulnerable groups at high risk of facing economic crisis.

The reason the Saffron Revolution is so significant is that after a towering rally on the August 8, 1988, which resulted in the army killing over 3000 people, people lived in fear under the control of the military junta.

How did Myanmar change? Despite the establishment of a civilian led government, Myanmar still has difficulties and lacks general safety. Government spending on health projects remained around $1.6 per capita in 2012. Even though Myanmar is currently under a coup, eventually democracy will prevail as it has in so many other countries in the world, ultimately reaching a totalizing effect.

The international response to Myanmar is worth noting. The Council of the European Union announced that they will be renewing sanctions against Myanmar, including an embargo on arms, asset freezes and travel limitations for officials. Indonesia's Foreign Minister argued that the sanctions should not be put into practice since they only harm the people that the EU is trying to help. This degree of sanctions also leads to increasing pressures from international businesses for the government to lift or decrease sanctions. This is often viewed as a debate between whether human rights should be chosen (assuming the sanctions are effective in this respect) over a free trade agreement that might release the tension between the Myanmar government and the international community.

When we are evaluating economic policies like these ones, it is imperative to measure their effectiveness. Firstly, sanctions are already in place, and there is no noticeable effect on the government. The prime minister responded to the sanction, which is already in place, by blaming the UN for the stagnant economic growth of the country. There was an election in 2010, partly due to the Revolution, which can be viewed as the government's response to the sanctions, so further sanctions increase should be reconsidered. Moreover, the western sanctions on Myanmar encourage the country to get closer to China and India as both are strong emerging economies within the region. This would decrease western influence within the region in conjunction with giving leverage for the EU to demand proper human rights treatment.

So, are the western sanctions the main contributor to Myanmar's poor situation? The answer is no. According to the International Bar Association, 95% of foreign investment is in the oil and gas sectors, which contribute almost zero to the employment market in Myanmar. There is also a lack of transparency in capital inflow, which appears to bypass governmental budgets. The main reason why Myanmar's government is to blame for its stagnant economic growth is that it has no intention of making Myanmar a business-friendly environment, nor of utilizing the oil sector's profit to improve living standards and education. It would be smart for the EU to consider setting political benchmarks for Myanmar to achieve under the current status quo.

Chinese Stock Market Turbulence (2015-2016)

What happened? A total of forty million stock accounts were opened between June 2014 and May 2015. China's stock market increased about 150% within a year, reaching the ceiling on June 12, 2015, and crashing with a bubble burst. The Shanghai Composite index fell by 5.9% within a week, and we must note that the 2015-2016 stock market boom in China was distinct from those that preceded it. The previous one, between 2005 and 2007, was due to the rapid growth of the Chinese economy as a whole. The difference amid the two is that the second time, people were trading on margin, meaning they used borrowed money to invest.

What caused the stock market bubble? As the economy of Mainland China was cooling down, the boom in the stock market became a medicine that stimulated domestic demand. Coupled with the loose monetary policy and the extensive opening of new investment opportunities, people opened accounts and entered the market. However, the lack of supervision made Chinese stocks a ticking time bomb. Just within a few weeks, the value of shares in the market accelerated at an incredible pace. Companies with merger earnings were seeing a significant rise in their shares while China's economy was going in the opposite direction. China's economy has been declining for the past couple of years, and it is predicted by many institutions, such as RaboResearch, that it will remain so for a few more years to come.

How did the government respond? During the week of the stock market turbulence, the political leaders made no responses to the crisis and avoided questions about it. There was an increase in high profile investigations of market manipulation, and various arrests of journalists that "fabricated rumors" about the financial situation in China. At least from a governmental perspective, we should be questioning whether systemic corruption is the reason for market failure, but the Chinese government did nothing like that. Later on, the Chinese government utilized limitations on short selling, encouraging mutual funds to purchase stocks.

The Anti-Extradition Law Amendment Bill Movement (2019-2020)

What happened? In 2019, a protest began in Hong Kong in response to the Extradition Law Amendment Bill proposed by the Chinese government. The Extradition Law Amendment Bill sparked Hong Kong citizen's anger towards the Chinese government since it was viewed as an attempt to extend its power towards the democratic and autonomous Hong Kong. This Bill essentially exposed Hong Kong citizens to unjust treatment and gave China a great amount of power over Hong Kong, limiting freedom of speech along with anything that could go against the Chinese government. The first protest was triggered back in April 2019. A series of protests forced the Hong Kong government to pause discussion on the Bill but they did not achieve its removal. People in Hong Kong were fearful that the bill would eventually be revived. Consequently, up to 1.7 million people, a quarter of the population, took to the street to protest. Protestors also assembled the Five Demands, which included: not characterizing protestors as rioters, the immediate release of protestors, legal inquiry towards police brutality, universal suffrage, and withdrawal of the bill. Finally, on September 4, 2019, the government announced the official withdrawal of the Bill, but completely dismissed the other four requests.

What was the content of the Bill? We need to be mindful of the fact that Hong Kong adopted One Country, Two System arrangement ever since 1997. Since then, they have had distinct political, socioeconomic, and legal arrangements with China for the past fifty years without change. The existing extradition bill in Hong Kong purposefully did not include the PRC into the conversation. However, the Extradition Law Amendment Bill would allow the Hong Kong government to send criminal suspects, in accordance with the petitions of any country, including the PRC. This means that the PRC would basically have the ability to accuse anyone in Hong Kong and exercise its legal right to sentence the criminal. Many view this as China basically ignoring the One Country, Two System policy, thus causing mass protests among different parts of Hong Kong.

How would the Extradition Law impact Hong Kong's Economy (Short Term)? During the protest, major banks suspended branch services, causing Hong Kong's equity benchmark, the Heng Seng Index, to show a mass decrease of 1.5%. Tourism income also decreased between 5% and 10%. One important thing to note is that along with the decrease in tourists, the Hong Kong International Airport suffered a $76 million loss from flight cancellations.

How would the Extradition Law impact Hong Kong's Economy (Long Term)? Due to the mass protests, the financial district shut down for a few days. Regarding long term effects, we can look at the statement released by the Hong Kong General Chamber of Commerce in which they heavily opposed the passing of the Extradition Bill, stating that the it would decrease the attractiveness of Hong Kong as a trading center for foreign business since it functioned differently and independently from the PRC. Hong Kong's reputation as a free and open financial center within the region would be jeopardized. The importance of this should be self-explanatory when considering the current trade agreements between Hong Kong and other countries like the United States. Hong Kong's autonomous status would become invalid under the Extradition Bill, making the trade arrangement between the US and Hong Kong illegitimate as well. The $67 billion bilateral trade between both sides would be heavily affected. Political freedom and a strong rule of law were the determining factors behind Hong Kong's reputation as the international banking and finance center. No matter what Hong Kong's future will be, it is certain that along with COVID-19, it is at risk of a long term outflow of capital investments and could possibly face mass emigration.

What we can learn from it. This will be relatively focused on general lessons instead of economic suggestions. First, we need to take the status quo into consideration. The PRC continues to exert its influence in Hong Kong, neglecting the fact that its people do not view this reformation as normal, but as an enormous looming pressure from the PRC government. People in Hong Kong have access to freedom of speech and the internet, and as such, the PRC should refrain from viewing Hong Kong as they do all the other areas in China that just blindly follow their rule. We also see a trend within the protests, if someone is more economically stable they tend not to go to the protest and vice versa. These protests also exposed the housing prices and the economic burden that young people in Hong Kong must bear. Long term policies in Hong Kong favor the rich over the poor, to such an extent that Hong Kong tops the world in regards to the gap between the rich and poor. We can also take a look at social media platforms. Public opinion about the government massively circulated on social media and the Hong Kong government tried to suppress it with the help of the PRC. This only led to an even greater rebound reaction from the protestors as they consistently shifted between platforms. Modern technologies allow the spread of information within seconds, with protestors consistently sharing police brutality posts and catching the attention of journalists from all over the world; the PRC has then already lost control of the internet. Lastly, police brutality was one of the most controversial elements within the protests. In response to the Hong Kong protests, the government decided to use forceful measures which sparked violent events between police and protestors. This acted as a fuel for the protests to take to the streets for an even longer period of time. When governments respond to people's manifestations it is imperative that violent measures are not carried out. These are the lessons we can learn from this event in order to attain stable and sustainable solutions towards conflicts like this one.

Chapter III: Europe

David Xu

The Russo-Japanese War (1904-1905)

Summary: The Russo-Japanese War was the military conflict between the Russian Empire and Japanese Empire over the control of Manchuria (currently North-eastern China) and the Korean Peninsula. The War ended with the Russian Empire's defeat in 1905. The Russo-Japanese War is highly significant due to various facts: it trumped the oriental belief of European superiority; It showcased the Japanese Empire's relatively high level of modernity and hinted at its imperial ambition, the dominating factor of the Southeast Asian theater during World War II; and it exhibited the Russian Empire's internal instability which later led to the Russian civil war.

Background of the War: Throughout the late 19th to early 20th century, the Qing Dynasty (currently China) was plagued with corruption and a fragile military. Qing was very much on the edge of collapse during this time and was defeated on numerous humiliating occasions by the British Empire amidst the First (1839-1842) and Second Opium War (1858-1869). Later on, the Qing also suffered greatly at the hands of the Allied forces (a conglomerate of eight nations) in the Boxer Rebellion (1900). This presented an opportunity for both the Russian and Japanese Empire who wished to expand their reign of influence on the now crumbling Asian Empire.

Japanese imperial Ambition: The Japanese Empire had long-held imperial ambitions over the then Chinese controlled Korean Peninsula. The Japanese Empire first eliminated Korea's protectorate status with the *First Japan-Korea Treaty of 1876*. Korea was granted a status of independence and allowed Japanese trading and extraterritorial rights within the Korea Peninsula. Japan's temporary influence was later undone during Korea's mutiny, after which Qing seized the opportunity to reinstate its rule. Throughout the 1880s, the Japanese Empire made several failed attempts to control Korea via the staging of domestic revolutions.

Sino-Japanese War (1894-1895): In 1894, the Qing dynasty mobilized troops at the request of the Korean monarch to assist them in suppressing a peasantry revolution. Citing a violation of the *Treaty of Tientsin* (1885) which stated that no Qing nor Japanese troops could operate in Korea, Japan seized the opportunity to deploy troops in the Korean Peninsula. As Japanese forces quickly took control of the Peninsula and continuously pushed northwards into Liaodong Peninsula, the First Sino-Japanese War (1894) broke out. Qing was in no shape to stand its ground and quickly admitted defeat to Japan in 1895. Signing the *Treaty of Shimonoseki*, Qing surrendered control of the Korean Peninsula, Liaodong Peninsula and Taiwan to Japan. This move was quickly objected to and later overturned by the intervention of Germany, France and Russia. Russia held enormous imperial interests and ambition in the Liaodong Peninsula. In Korea, Russia leveraged the civil unrest and the allegations directed at Emperor Gojong of Korea, to successfully prop up a Russian friendly government.

Russian's imperial ambition: Under the *Treaty of Aigun* of 1858, later reinforced by the Beijing Convention of 1860, Alexander III led the Russian Empire's first expansionist policy into Asia. Territories north of Amur and a portion of the Ussuri maritime region were ceded to the Qing dynasty, which included what later became the port city of Vladivostok. Yet, Russia's shipping center in Vladivostok, Siberia was not suitable for operation during winter. Seeking to reinforce its maritime capability for both its trade and naval operations, Russia leased Port Arthur on the Liaodong Peninsula from the Qing Dynasty in 1897. This need for maritime access is one of the first instances when the Russian Empire's expansionist ambition into East Asia transpired into actions under Tzar Nicholas II and truly worried the now emerging Japanese Empire.

In 1899 the Russian Empire along with seven other nations dispatched numerous troops to suppress the Boxer Rebellion and stage a permanent presence in the Liaodong peninsula. This move was viewed by Japan as a direct threat against its imperial interest within the region. In 1904, the Japanese Empire attempted to negotiate a non-aggression pact with the Russian Empire. The former requested Russian's recognition of its rule over Korea. In exchange, the latter would receive Japanese support for their influence over Manchuria. However, Russia saw the need to establish a buffer state along the 39th parallel, a demand that was perceived as a direct threat to Japanese imperial ambition in mainland Asia. Hence, the Sino-Japanese War of 1904 began.

Outcome of the War: Japan's victory shocked the world, considering their relatively underdeveloped status some decades before. Additionally, it must be stated that there was a level of racially motivated orientalist prejudice because the international community deemed it impossible for an Asian country to achieve anything significant, let alone, defeating a European empire. Nonetheless, Japan had conducted extensive political and economic reforms in the previous decades, known as the Meiji Restoration. Furthermore, to prevent the recurrence of the triple intervention, Japan allied itself prior to the war. These moves combined really tipped the scale in Japan's favor.

Japan's success story: The Meiji Restoration is generally referred to the period of extensive political and economic reforms under the reign of Emperor Meiji (明治) from 1868-1912. The Meiji Restoration is an attempt to appease the revolution and restore peace and stability within the then highly divided Japanese society. Prior to the Meiji era, the Empire was largely under the governance of Tokugawa shogunate (military governance). This was known as the Edo period, which ended the warring state, but in the process largely reduced the Japanese monarchy to no more than a figurehead.

The Tokugawa shogunate ruled with a heavy fist and followed a strict class system which resulted in the rebellion of many within the

Daimyo class, and later transpired into the Boshin War (1868-1869). The Boshin War concluded with the imperial victory. Emperor Meiji had his power restored, and his cabinet office quickly constituted a series of reforms (Westernization). These reforms include public education, abolishment of the feudal system and the creation of a westernized national army. Thus, began the emergence of the Japanese Empire in Asia.

Russia's Defeat: Besides Japanese success in rapidly modernizing a century prior, the Russian Empire's problematic strategy is also to blame for its failure in the War. Before the War began, Tzar Nicholas II was convinced that he was guaranteed a victory. However, the bulk of the Russian force and resources were concentrated in Eastern Europe. Comparatively, the Japanese Empire had fought the Sino-Japanese War just a decade ago and as a result were considerably more experienced and prepared in operating in the regions.

Russian's military forces experienced a humiliating setback at the beginning of the War. The Russian troops, despite its substantial size, were quickly surrounded in the Port of Arthur. Tzar Nicholas II directed its force to be quickly transferred from its Eastern European outposts through both its Trans-Siberian railway and its Baltic Fleet. The ground troops quickly arrived but were defeated. The Baltic Fleet had a chaotic voyage due to its inexperience. Friendly fire was a common scene, including the firing of a British fleet that the Russians mistook for Japanese, this episode is known as the Dogger Bank Incident. The majority of the fleet were instructed to avoid Suez and to travel through the Good Hope, Cape Town, causing their months' late arrival. This is just one of the incidents exposing the relative ineffectiveness of Russian Troops during the War. This conflict promptly concluded after the Battle of Tsushima where the Russian fleet suffered a two-third casualty.

Aftermath: With US President Theodore Roosevelt acting as the mediator, Russia and Japan signed the "Treaty of Portsmouth" whereby Russian handed over control to Japan of the Liaodong Peninsula, including Port Arthur, and officially recognized Japanese influence in the Korean Peninsula. Roosevelt was awarded a Nobel Peace Prize for his role in brokering peace in the Russo-Japanese War. The humiliating defeat quickly escalated into peasant civil unrest in Russia. Although quickly suppressed, it arguably provided a blueprint for the communist revolution a decade later. After successfully securing triumph against the Russian Empire, the Japanese continued its expansionist policy in Asia, setting the stage for the eventuality of the Second World War in the pacific theater.

British Foreign Policy and Defence Strategy Post-Brexit (2016-Present)

On June 23, 2016, the British public shocked the world with the highly consequential referendum result, 52% to 48% in favor of the country's withdrawal of its membership from the European Union(i.e. Brexit) (BBC, 2016). The outcome of the 2016 referendum effectively ended Britain's status and its decades-long influential role as a member of the political and economic union of Europe. The then-Prime Minister David Cameron, a firm remainer (i.e. Supporter of the UK remaining in the EU.) resigned over his failure to promote Britain's remain campaign. Most importantly, the question regarding Britain's future within the European Union also conditioned and dictated the British political landscape. As a result of Britain's unprecedented decision, the United Kingdom underwent two rounds of elections, the latest one in 2019, that resulted in a dominating victory of the Conservative Party, compared to other parties.

The 2019 general election, also known as the 'Brexit election', was a hugely influential strategic move by the current Prime Minister Boris Johnson to break the deadlock within the British legislature in the hope of consolidating a majority to pass his Brexit deal with the European Union. The election resulted in a landslide victory for the

Conservative Party, securing a majority of 365 seats in the British parliament. (i.e. House of Commons) (BBC, 2019). The Labour Party leader, Jeremy Corbyn, resigned after this humiliating defeat in the hands of the conservatives. Many observers believe that this decision was justified since Corbyn did not provide the desperately needed leadership in this election, considering that the Labour Party failed to provide a definitive stand on Brexit (i.e. to either leave or remain). Instead, they proposed that another referendum should be summoned.

As a firm Brexiter, Johnson argued that Brexit would allow Britain to take back its sovereignty. With the Conservative Party securing a dominating majority in Parliament, it was inherently crucial for the Johnson administration to outline the direction of British foreign policy post-Brexit. To fulfill Johnson's Brexit narrative, the Secretary of State for Foreign Affairs, Commonwealth & Development Office (FCDO) Dominic Rabb, introduced a new foreign policy strategy, named the 'Global Britain'. Raab highlighted three major pillars of the 'Global Britain': 1) Britain as an ally in Europe; 2) Britain as a 'Champion' for free trade and 3) Britain as a force for good in the world (Raab, 2020). But how do these translate into action?

On March, 16, 2021, the Cabinet Office of the United Kingdom released its long anticipated integrated review (IR)titled 'A Global Britain in a Competitive Age' (British Cabinet Office, 2021). This review outlined the UK's strategies for security, defense, foreign policy, and development. The IR was the first comprehensive strategic review of the post-Brexit era under the vision of a Global Britain. Notably, the strategy places heavy emphasis on science and technology (S&T) and the Indo-pacific (Grevatt, 2021).

IR is a periodic government assessment of both the UK's current capacity and the future strategic environment based on existing trends in the international community. In the IR, Britain recognizes the existing nature of 'strategic competition' that resulted from the revisionist effort in challenging the existing international order. As it stands, Britain poses the ambition to shape an open international order for the future. But, the reality of Britain's position as a middle power also concedes the ambitious goal of the UK in attempting to significantly alter strategic competition.

One must first look at what Britain's national interests are. In the IR, the government shortlisted: sovereignty, security and prosperity as the three core national interests. Sovereignty highlighted the need to protect Britain's democratic process free from coercion or interference, rather than traditional concerns. In addition to conventional security concerns and the need to prevent terrorism, this strategy highlighted the need to safeguard Britain's critical national infrastructures (CNI), an effort to preserve Britain's democratic institutions and way of life. Prosperity focused on the economic wellbeing of the nation and it views Brexit as an opportunity for Britain to promote international trade on its own terms.

The increasing emphasis on S&T is rather simple for Britain. It will defend Britain's interest in all five operation domains and grant the upper hand in shaping international order for the future, in the greater context of constant systematic competition. Britain's emphasis on S&T can be divided into two sections: the need to equip and to protect. Regarding defence issues and given the existing instability, there is an urgent need to better equip Britain's armed forces. This means an increase in not only conventional nuclear deterrence but also modernizing existing forces. This implies that Britain will provide all branches of its forces with better conventional equipment and the integration of technology, including the use of digital technologies in frontline operations. The package also includes £6.6 billion investment for the MOD research project. Secondly, there is the call for protecting Britain's interest against foreign adversaries. Based on current relations, Britain will adapt 'own-contribute-access' approaches to critical CNI development in enhancing British S&T power. Needless to say, given the existing competition in the field of 5G telecommunication, this decision will not be positively received by leading non-western states in this field. (Bloomberg, 2021)

The need for military modernization is recognized by IR and overall positively received. Yet, it should be noted that many of the objectives outlined in the IR were first addressed by Sir Richard Barrons in 2014 (Barrons& Lawson 2016). Presently, the notion of acquiring strategic superiority through S&T, stated in the IR, will be unlikely at best. Besides the need to address the defence concern in the cyber domain, the IR did not specify in detail the way in which Britain is planning on enhancing the S&T aspect of the UK's defence capacity. From what was said, praises were given for the emphasis on S&T and urged the need to revolutionize Britain's existing defence (Mehdian-Staffell, 2021).

The emphasis on Indo-Pacific relations, a highly competitive region and one of high significance to British security, was also recognized as a growing concern for the coming decade. By nature, this conceptualization of the Indo-Pacific region will create a paradox for London. This paradox was rightfully highlighted, stating a need to compete and cooperate with those who do not share Britain's value, sometimes even at the same time. This sets the undertone of the overall British vision on the Indo-Pacific region: a strategic ambiguity. The need to compromise was clearly underpinned in Britain's Indo-Pacific strategy from the very beginning.

To address the UK's strategic approaches to the Indo-Pacific region, China is most certainly the crucial focus. As expected, the IR no longer holds an optimistic view compared with previous reviews (SDSR-15) (British Cabinet Office, 2015). In the IR, the UK views China as a human rights violator, a systematic competitor, while it remains a crucial trading partner. This places the UK in an awkward position; one that will not likely be favourable in the long run. On the one hand, Britain will have to find a way to navigate this relation, while honoring agreements with Hong Kong, in which Britain promised to protect the BNO passport holder. Additionally, a close trading relationship with China will not be positively perceived by regional allies, but rather as a constraint on Britain. On the other hand, China does not appreciate the meddling in its internal affairs and will likely curb any unwanted interest. Australia is one of the most recent examples (Bloomberg, 202). Given the intensification of strategic competition among high-volume trading powers, the UK will need to establish a clearer and more sustainable approach to the nature of its relations with China.

Finally, the military aspect of the UK's Indo-Pacific approach, outlined the need for further multilateral security cooperation with regional allies. Focusing specifically on pursuing the freedom of navigation rights, the UK is hoping to avoid possible choke points and establish a constant military presence within the region. Considering the UK's existing focus on the Euro-Atlantic region, the newly heightened focus on the Indo-pacific one will likely put the UK's finite resources to a test. Britain's reliance on US logistic support for the HMS Queen Elizabeth maiden deployment into the Indo-Pacific region (Chutter, 2021) (a maneuver intended to show the UK's defence posture and which resulted in its failure to produce a carrier strike group) is the very testament of that.

The UK's long-awaited defence review is not satisfactory. It did a fair job in recognizing the existing shortcomings of the UK's capacity and provided some accommodations to the issues raised. What the IR did was summarize existing strategic challenges, but it should have provided a better assessment of the strategic environment for the future, as it was originally intended. That being said, the UK's emphasis on the Indo-Pacific region was much needed. Yet the division of finite resources into two geostrategic hot spots will pose a serious challenge. In the same fashion, the IR failed to provide a long-term strategic approach to existing stakeholders in the region. Overall, this review feels very much like a post-great power's unrealistic hope of reliving its past glory under the new banner of a 'Global Britain'

Chapter IV: Latin America & the Caribbean

Isabela de Almeida Godoy

The Mexican Revolution (1910-1924)

Revolutions do not just start themselves. For an event to be referred to as a revolution it must first be an explosive response to a deep internal issue. In Mexico's case, it was the Porfiriato, the period from 1876 to 1911 in which Porfirio Díaz was president. This thirty-one-year dictatorial regime excluded and impoverished the population, giving way for powerful local leaders to revolt against him and his rule in a civil war that lasted seven years and fourteen armed conflicts, until the establishment of a new constitution in 1917.

The trigger of the Revolution: The 1910 Mexican presidential election had Porfirio Díaz and Francisco Madero as the two main candidates. Díaz's victory marked his seventh term in a row, leaving the political opposition once again frustrated. Wanted for rebellion by the government, Madero self-exiled in Texas, from where he wrote the *Plan of San Luis de Potosí* (*Plan de San Luis*, in Spanish). This document denounced Porfirio's regime and urged the peasantry's support, who, in turn, were led by the two leaders that would become the epitomical faces of liberty in the country: Emiliano Zapata and Francisco "Pancho" Villa.

Rebel victory: In 1911 rebels took control over major regions of the country, ending once and for all the Porfiriato and making Madero president. The main reason for the population's rage during Porfirio Díaz's rule stemmed from land distribution, however, this was not properly addressed while Madero was in office before his assassination in 1913. Madero was succeeded in the presidency by one of his generals, Victoriano Huerta, who established another dictatorship and unleashed the need for revolutionaries to take matters into their own hands once again. As a result, the Constitutional Army (Ejército constitucionalista), was formed with the objective of re-establishing constitutionality and lawfulness in the country. Rebel groups fought against the government until Huerta renounced in 1914. It was also around that time when the United States invaded the city of Veracruz and imposed an arms embargo on Huerta's regime. In the wake of these events, Venustiano Carranza became president and gave the country a new constitution in 1917.

Repercussions: The Mexican Revolution was one of the bloodiest events in all of modern Latin American history, having caused the death of 2 million Mexicans. All revolutionary leaders were also assassinated: Madero in 1913, Zapata in 1919, Carranza in 1920, Villa in 1923 and Obregón in 1928. The greatest objective of the Revolution, land reform, however, was achieved, even if only partially.

Argentinian Peronism (1946-1976)

Peronism (or Peronismo in Spanish) refers to the populist phenomenon started by Juan Domingo Perón, who served as president of Argentina from 1946 to 1952, 1952 to 1955 and again from 1973 to 1976.

Early years of the movement: The military coup of 1943 marked the end of a dark and conservative era for Argentina. At this time, Perón occupied various high-ranking positions within the revolutionary government, but it was only in 1945 that the fate of the country began to take shape. Perón had built a positive reputation for himself among the population, yet when the revolutionary regime began to crumble, the military decided to sacrifice Perón. He was not only forced to step down, but also arrested. The working class led historical protests against his arrest, obtained his freedom and consolidated the movement that had been named after him: Peronism.

The Golden Era: The first few years of Perón's government represented the ascension of the working class to power and, although he had been elected by the people, Perón never failed to define his government as revolutionary, setting himself up to be one of the most paradigmatic names of Latin America's populism phenomenon. It was a period of economic independence, political sovereignty and social justice for the country through many social and market reforms. The GDP grew 8% and internal consumption 14% per year.

Eva Perón: At the height of Peronism and the creation of the Peronist Party, the figure of Juan Perón's second and then-current wife, María Eva Duarte de Perón, began to shine among the population. She was a very participative first lady and embodied the ascension of women onto mainstream politics in the country. Eva engaged directly with the people and took a number of matters into her own hands in order to improve the healthcare system, increase universal education and advance women's rights. In a nutshell, Eva became the charisma and face of the movement while Juan was its firm leader.

Crisis: The early 1950s saw a tragic downfall of the structures of Peronism. An economic crisis made Perón's efforts harder to continue the steady prosperity of the country and, in the wake of new elections, the population started a movement of their own demanding that Eva would run for vice-president with her husband in hopes of making her participation in the government official. Eva renounced her candidature in 1951, the same year she became aware of a tumor that would lead to her passing in July 1952. This marked one of the greatest moments of grief for Argentina to date.

The fall: Following the worsening of the economic crisis and the death of the Peronist movement's charismatic leader, Perón struggled to maintain an image of stability for the country. His popularity, although very high, was slowly descending, while a strong political opposition started to rise. In 1955, while he took part in a rally in Plaza de Mayo, an airstrike (ordered by the navy) terrorized the crowd, killing 364 civilians. This was the coup attempt that led Perón to seek refuge in Uruguay, where he stayed until 1973.

Return to Argentina and repercussions: The following years were very unstable for Argentina. While Perón's government had been a symbol of hope and prosperity for the country, the coming years saw two more military coups, one in 1962 and one in 1966, which established a brutal military dictatorship in the country until its fall in 1973. This last dictatorship crumbled after the Peronist party and movement (which by then carried the name of Judicialist Party, Partido Judicialista in Spanish) pressured for the return of democracy and of Perón. Juan Perón returned to Argentina with his new wife Isabel, who took office in 1974, when Perón passed away. Notwithstanding, two years later, in 1976, antiperonist forces struck with yet another coup, leading to another military dictatorship that would last until 1983. Although the period from the 1940s to the 1980s was very turbulent for Argentinian politics and economy, the legacy of Peronism is still tangible among the population through neoperonism and Perón's Justicialist Party, which is currently in power in the country.

The Cuban Revolution (1953-1959)

The Cuban Revolution was one of the most relevant events of the 20th century, it also represented the height of the Cold War, and it changed the fate of the small Caribbean island forever.

The Batista Dictatorship: Fulgencio Batista was a member of the military, a key figure in the 1933 Revolution and president from 1940 to 1944. At the end of the 1940s, he decided to get back into politics, but when he came to the realization that he could not obtain the needed amount of support to win the elections democratically, he staged a coup against president Prío Socarrás in 1952. He managed this because he joined forces with the military and had the backing of the government of the United States. This was the beginning of a dictatorship that would last until 1959.

The Beginning of the Revolution: Opposition to Batista's regime began soon after it was established. In 1953, Fidel Castro and his men attempted to take over military bases on the island, but were detained by Batista. Once he was released from prison, Castro founded the 26th of July Movement (Movimiento 26 de Junio in Spanish, also known as M-26-7) which was intended to overthrow Batista's rule. In 1955, Castro self-exiled to Mexico, where he and his men regrouped and prepared to properly begin the revolution. In 1956, they were once again arrested, this time in Mexico, under suspicion of communist conspiracy, but were freed soon after. He then returned to Cuba, where himself and eighty-two more men began to forcefully oppose Batista's regime. The 26th of July Movement would go on to gain support, although slowly, from the local population, which helped them to progressively take control of the island.

Victorious Revolution: After years of guerrilla warfare, the revolutionaries would come out victorious when, on the last day of 1958, Batista fled the country while rebel troops successfully took over Havana. As the Revolution drew to a close, Fulgencio Batista received asylum in Spain, where he passed away in 1973, and Fidel Castro became the leader of the Cuban Republic.

Installment of the Rebel Government: Now in power, Castro began a number of reforms with the objective of reversing Batista's policies and installing a regime aligned with the guiding principles of the Revolution. During a critical moment in the Cold War, Castro strengthened relations with the Soviet Union, obtaining support from the Communist International (Comitern) to rebuild the island and set acute market and social reforms in place. These reforms would induce Cuba's reputation as a global reference in health and education.

The Missile Crisis and the Embargo: The Missile Crisis can be defined as the uppermost moment of tension of the Cold War, when the United States and the Soviet Union were the closest to engaging in direct warfare. After a coup attempted by CIA-trained counter-revolutionaries in Cuba, Castro decided to let the Soviet Union install a nuclear missile base on the island, which was of major strategic importance. The discovery of these missiles by the United States led to a diplomatic crisis that had the potential to become a full-blown nuclear war. Negotiation between the USSR and the US resolved the conflict under the condition that the Soviet Union removed the missiles and the US did not further endeavor to forcefully take control over Cuba's government. Months before the crisis, the United States extended the embargo they had imposed on the island in 1960 to almost all exports, seeking the suffocation of the Cuban economy. The embargo became increasingly problematic for the island after the dissolution of the USSR in 1992. It is the longest-lasting trading embargo in modern history, and it is still in place, greatly shaping Cuban economy to this day.

The Brazilian Military Dictatorship (1964-1985)

On March 31, 1964, democratically elected Brazilian president João "Jango" Goulart was forced out of office by a US-backed military coup d'état. What followed was twenty-one-years of military dictatorship that caused thousands of civilian's deaths, disappearances and broken families. During this period, instead of a regime where power was controlled and administered by a single person, there were five different men who held the presidential title, all of which were high ranking members of the military: Humberto Castelo Branco (1964-1967), Artur Costa e Silva (1967-1969), Emílio Médici (1969-1974), Ernesto Giesel (1974-1979) and João Figueiredo (1979-1985).

Context of the Coup: In 1961, a mere seven months into his term, democratically elected Jânio Quadros resigned from the presidency in a frustrated attempt of "political articulation" giving way for his vice-president, João Goulart, to take office. The sudden change was not well-received by the Brazilian elites given the fact that the new president had leftist tendencies and focused most of his policies on base reforms, particularly, land reforms, which were much feared by the powerful landowners of the country. Internationally, the supposed advancement of communist ideals in Brazil also led the United States Central Intelligence Agency (CIA), amidst the Cold War and the Cuban Revolution, to interfere in the country in the coup of 1964, orchestrated by the Brazilian armed forces with the support of civilian elite groups.

Increased Repression: Throughout the twenty-one-year dictatorship, the presidents would enact Atos Institucionais (AI), or institutional acts, decrees in which federal power and civilian repression were greatly increased. Indirect elections were imposed, all political parties were wiped out, and measures of censorship were applied. The most brutal of those institutional acts, known as AI5, was enacted by Costa e Silva in 1968, which brought about the closure of congress indefinitely, imposed national martial law, and gave the government the right to severely punish political opponents. This was the bleakest moment of the regime.

Relaxation of the Regime: Over a decade of dictatorship later, the armed forces were progressively unable to maintain such severe and centralized repression, giving way to a process of gradual loosening of the regime during Giesel's and Figueiredo's terms. The economic prosperity seen in the early 1970s came at the expense of an external debt of 12.5 billion dollars, growth in inflation and poverty rates, leading to a massive wave of protests and labor strikes in light of the economic crisis that followed. In 1979, the Lei da Anistia, or Amnesty Law, was passed, allowing political prisoners to be freed and asylum seekers to return to the country, while also granting forgiveness to members of the police and military that participated in acts of torture.

In 1984 during the Diretas Já demonstration, civilians demanded direct elections in the country. Despite that, in 1985, Tancredo Neves, the first president to not be a member of the military since 1964, was indirectly elected by congress, pinpointing the end of the Brazilian military dictatorship. In 1988, the current Constitution of Brazil was drafted, substituting the one imposed by the regime in 1967.

The Chilean Military Dictatorship (1973-1990)

Pinochet's regime was one of the most brutal ever faced by a Latin American country in the 20th century. For seventeen years Chileans were under a rough authoritarian government that murdered and incarcerated thousands. This period was also defined by the institution of ultraliberal market reforms, making Chile one of the biggest neoliberal laboratories for Global North nations to date.

Salvador Allende and the threat to the US's influence in America: In 1970 President Salvador Allende was democratically elected in Chile. He pertained to the traditional socialist left, and intended to promote heavy social, land and economic reforms in the country. Within the context of the Cold War, this posed an obvious threat to the United States influence in a continent where it had already lost a major area: Cuba. Due to this, three years later, on September 11, 1973, the CIA, along with the Chilean military and economic elites, carried out a coup, that resulted in Allende's suicide and the installment of a military regime led by Chief Commander of the armed forces Augusto Pinochet.

Civilian repression during the dictatorship: As soon as it was established, the dictatorship carried out many authoritarian measures such as censorship, mass incarceration of the opposition, torture and assassination. It is estimated that around 40,000 people fell victim to the regime, 3,000 of which were directly killed or went missing.

Chicago Boys and economic policy during the dictatorship: The Chicago Boys were a group of Chilean economists who, through a partnership between Chilean universities and the University of Chicago, were able to continue their studies at this United States university. There, they were exposed to the holy grail of the United States economy: liberalism. In the early 1970s, many of these economists were deeply dissatisfied with the path their country was following under Allende and began to write a new possible guidebook for economic policy for the country, known as *El Ladrillo*, or *The Brick*, due to its size. The coup of 1973 posed an opportunity for the Chicago Boys to return, and they were soon given high-ranking positions within Pinochet's ministry of economy. For the seventeen following years, Chilean economic policies were determined by them, guided by all that they had learned while in the United States. The lack of checks and balances of the dictatorship allowed them to implement unlimited ultraliberal measures, massively privatizing and liberalizing the economy, ultimately generating disastrous social consequences Chile faces to this day and that have been the reason for the recent civil unrest. Now, Chile is in the process of writing a new constitution that once and for all eliminates every single vestige of the legacy of Pinochet's dictatorship and, hopefully, promotes positive social change in the country.

The fall of the regime: Throughout the 1980s, despite state violence and the illegalization of the political opposition, leftist groups began to organize protests against the regime, demanding a switch towards democratization. Finally, in 1988, amidst pressure from the public, a plebiscite was summoned to decide whether the people wanted Pinochet to remain in power or not. With 56% of the votes, "no" won and the transition to democracy began in the country. Similar to the Brazilian case, an Amnesty Law was passed forgiving both the political establishment (the military, torturers and criminals of the regime) and the political opposition (those who had been incarcerated, prosecuted and exiled). Despite many national and international attempts to prosecute Pinochet on charges of murder, genocide and torture, he passed away in 2006, having never been held accountable for his crimes.

The Lost Decade (1980's)

The Lost Decade refers to an economic crisis in the 1980s, which was seen in most, if not all, countries in Latin America. It was a direct consequence of the authoritarian and neoliberal regimes in power and the 1970s oil crashes, which generated exorbitant foreign debts and skyrocketed inflation rates in most of the region. Most Latin American countries at the time were also struggling to maintain a fixed exchange rate in the face of a decaying international monetary system, which forced them to allow their currencies to fluctuate through deep monetary reform.

Brazil: In Brazil, the Lost Decade followed an "economic miracle" that took place between 1968 and 1973. During this period, the Gross Domestic Product grew by 11% every year and inflation lowered considerably, all at the cost of significant growth in the foreign debt. Essentially, the military government at the time was funding internal projects with money obtained overseas by making more flexible the entrance of multinational companies in the country, weakening worker unions and taking billionaire loans from international organizations. Although making for a seemingly stable economy, the economic miracle mostly favored the Brazilian economic elites, further deepening the gap between the rich and the poor. That means the economic growth did not translate into social impact. The economic burst began to slow down after the 1973 oil crash, becoming a full-blown economic crisis, the Lost Decade, later on. At the end of the military regime, in 1985, the foreign debt represented 54% of the GDP, four times more than it did before the 1964 coup, and inflation reached rates as high as 1782%.

Peru: Peru was particularly affected by the Lost Decade, for a number of reasons. The 1980s began after the fall of a leftist military regime, giving way for a democratic government that implemented neoliberal reforms, bringing the country further into a premeditated recession due to the high foreign debt and the crises of the 1970s. The 1980s were also the highest period of activity of the Sendero Luminoso, or the Shining Path, a Maoist-Marxist terrorist group that launched many attacks and orchestrated massacres frequently throughout the entire decade. The crisis in Peru led to significant growth in inflation and poverty rates. This generalized terror and instability would lead to the election of Alberto Fujimori in 1990. One could say that the Lost Decade in Peru would go on to last not ten, but thirty years, going from the 1970s up to the 2000s.

The Fuljimori Dictatorship in Peru (1990-2000)

The Fujimori dictatorship is one of, if not the last, explicitly authoritarian periods in Latin American history. It is also the only case of a country in this region that reverted to a dictatorship after having been democratized. Alberto Fujimori was elected in 1990, faced with a Peru destroyed by economic and social crises and the threat of the Shining Path, a terrorist group of Maoist-Marxist alignment which had launched several attacks and orchestrated multiple massacres throughout the 1980s. The organization was responsible for between 20,000 and 50,000 assassinations, from 1980 to 2000. All the while, the state claimed even more lives than the terrorists did during the counterterrorist war. Under Fujimori's dictatorial regime and at the threat of the Shining Path, Peruvians were caught between a rock and a hard place.

Election and the Autogolpe de Estado of 1992: Fujimori won the 1990 elections against Nobel-award winner Mario Vargas Llosa due to his image as a "savior" that seduced a crises-ridden country. The increased militarization of the country and the counterterrorist efforts led Fujimori to close congress and suspend the constitution in what would be known as the Autogolpe de Estado, or self-coup, of 1992. In practical terms, this granted Fujimori the ability to act as he pleased in all related-state affairs and considerably increase state violence against the Shining Path and any other form of political opposition.

Neoliberal reforms: One of the biggest characteristics of this period was Fujimori's approach to economic reforms which were deeply focused on neoliberalism and destatization. The Autogolpe allowed him to freely implement all reforms he desired and, by the end of 1996, he had already privatized over 130 state-owned companies as well as the social security pension system and part of the healthcare system. He also reverted the land reforms carried out throughout the 1970s. These market reforms, along with the successful, although bloody, counterterrorism efforts, allowed him an easy reelection in 1995.

Fall of Fujimori and trials: After a frustrated election in 2000, which the constitution did not allow him to evade, and having lost popularity among the electoral base, Fujimori fled to Japan and resigned his position as president. After being charged with multiple crimes, including murder, kidnapping, and crimes against humanity, congress ordered his extradition back. While Japan refused to extradite one of its own citizens, as he had dual citizenship, several other investigations were carried out against him during the early 2000s with no success in actually convicting him since he was never present in the trials. In 2006, he returned to Latin America with the intention of running for the Peruvian presidential elections of that year. Upon arriving in Chile, he was arrested and, by 2007, he was extradited back to Peru, where he was convicted of multiple human rights violations and is currently doing time.

Latin America's 'Pink Tide' (2000-Present)

The phenomenon known as the Latin American 'Pink Tide' (or 'Marea Rosa', in Spanish) refers to the simultaneous ascension of leftist governments in many countries in the region after the turn of the century, including: Argentina, Bolivia, Brazil, Chile, Ecuador, El Salvador, Guyana, Honduras, Mexico, Nicaragua, Paraguay, Peru, Saint Vincent, Suriname, Uruguay and Venezuela.

General background: The 20th century was a troubled period in Latin American history. Most countries faced brutal dictatorships with major United States intervention which led to the implementation of severe neoliberal policies. As it is known today, Latin America served as a liberalism laboratory for USA leaders. These experiments caused many economic catastrophes in the region. After years of right-wing liberal policies, the dawn of the 21st century allowed for leftist groups to snatch a space for themselves within Latin American politics, making it possible for left-wing leaders to be elected across the majority of the subcontinent for the first time in decades.

Argentina: The Pink Tide arrives in Argentina after a long period of crisis that had unleashed the piquetero movement, a series of protests and strikes in response to the high unemployment rates in the country. It is then that Néstor Kirchner is elected through the Justicialist Party, beginning the era of neoperonism. The region's commodity boom of the 2000s facilitated considerable economic prosperity for Argentina during his term. In 2007, his wife, Cristina Fernández, was elected. She went on to be re-elected in 2011. Nonetheless, the soy devaluation crisis in 2013 and 2014 festered the growth of liberal antiperonist opposition, leading Mauricio Macri to win the 2015 elections. That should have been the end of the Pink Tide in Argentina, but another economic crisis, in 2018 and 2019, blocked Macri's attempt at re-election, once again culminating the victory of the Justicialist Party in the federal elections, with Alberto Fernández as president and the recognizable Cristina Kirchner as vice-president.

Brazil: At the last stage of the military dictatorship, in 1980, the Partido dos Trabalhadores, PT (Worker's Party, in English), was founded. One of its founders was syndicate leader Luiz Inácio "Lula" da Silva. He won his first election in 2002, as the first left-wing president of the country since João Goulart in 1964. After completing his second term, he elected a successor, Dilma Rousseff, in 2011. She went on to win another term, however, a wave of protests in 2013 and 2014 began to weaken PT's comfortable control over Brazilian politics, and gave way for the forgotten yet traditional right to get back on the playing field. Rousseff was impeached in 2016, in what would be later considered to be an institutional coup. Her vice-president, Michel Temer, who belonged to the traditional right-wing party MDB, went on to finish her term. The erosion of Brazilian democracy and institutions that had begun in 2013 paved the way for far-right politician Jair Bolsonaro to be elected in 2018, marking the end of the Pink Tide in Brazil. Under Bolsonaro, Brazil completes its eighth year of political instability.

Bolivia: Like in Brazil and Argentina, the surge in left-wing politics in Bolivia came after years of implementation of neoliberal policies. However, Morales' victory in the 2005 elections is particularly relevant as he was Bolivia's first and, as of now, only indigenous president in a country made up of over 60% native population. Despite the many advances in pro-indigenous policies he implemented in the country, many of the previously established neoliberal policies remained in place causing continuous conflict among indigenous communities. Bolivia saw a lot of economic prosperity under his government, which focused its efforts on indigenous rights and the war on drugs which had been imposed through the influence of the United States years prior. While Morales remained popular for thirteen years, it was still a long cycle for one leader to govern a country, which made the right-wing political elites very dissatisfied. The 2019 elections were very turbulent for the country and claims of electoral fraud were widespread. Despite having technically won the election, he resigned to the presidency and was offered political asylum in Mexico. He returned to the country almost a year later after Luis Arce, who belonged to MAS (Morales' political party), was sworn into office, making the clear statement that his presence in Bolivian politics is far from over.

The traditional left versus the Pink Tide left: Despite being a surge of left-wing governments in the region, the Pink Tide phenomenon is not necessarily aligned with the leftist leaders and movements that existed in Latin America prior to the wave of right-wing dictatorships. While the traditional Latin American left was revolutionary, communist and refused to form alliances with center and right-wing politics, this newer left is institutionalist at its core and highly influenced by the neoliberal policies massively implemented during the 1980s and 1990s. This, in practical terms, marks a fragmentation between these two distinct left generations, which could account for the retraction of the Pink Tide during the past years.

The Venezuelan Crisis (2013-Present)

During the 1980s to the 1990s, global oil prices fell drastically which caused Venezuela's economy to contract significantly. There have been various instances of hyperinflation, the spread of disease and an extremely high poverty rate in Venezuela. The country's inflation was up to 10000% in 2019. Once considered the richest nation in Latin America, with its enormous oil reserves that even surpass Saudi Arabia's to this very day, Venezuela now suffers a collapse in its national economy.

Venezuelan economy before the crisis: Venezuela saw great economic prosperity for much of the 20th century due to its enormous oil reserves. This economic bliss enabled the rise of a very rich elite who, from the get-go, spent exorbitant amounts of money internationally. That was a testament to the lifestyle of Venezuelan elites at the time, who were known to live lavishly. Although those were signs of a growing and prosperous country, it is known that internal investment, essential for the development of a country's economy, was neither promoted by the government nor by civil society at the time. That, jointly with the fact that the whole of Venezuela's profit came from a sole source, oil, would lead to the collapse of the economy.

Beginning of the turbulence: While the oil crash of 1973 served as a clear display of power from the Organization of the Petroleum Exporting Countries, of which Venezuela is an important member, the 1980s and 1990s saw a drastic fall in petroleum prices. This fact greatly impacted all OPEC countries, but Venezuela became the most gravely affected due to its nearly nonexistent industry. Up until that point, the country imported almost all products it consumed and even the oil industry was underdeveloped. The drop in oil prices, then, caused the economy to implode.

Generalized socio-economic crisis: After Venezuela's leader, Hugo Chávez, who was first elected in 1999, died in 2013, his successor, Nicolás Maduro, took office. Despite the increasing crisis in the country, Chávez was able to maintain a high popularity among the population through both his social policies and his charismatic personality. Maduro's image, however, is much colder and distant. This change in government and the embargo imposed by the United States since 2014 has driven Venezuela to one of the worst humanitarian crises in the world. Extreme poverty went from 10% to 85% from

2014 to 2018, economic activity has contracted 65% from 2013 to 2019 and nearly 10 million people have escaped the country.

How did the government respond? In response to hyperinflation, Maduro's government devalued its currency, the bolivar, by 150% and pegged it to the pretro instead of the dollar. The pretro is a cryptocurrency developed earlier by Maduro himself that enjoys the backing of state-owned oil reserves. However, the pretro is viewed as an ineffective currency and, as such, it was fruitless in stabilizing the economy. Efforts made by the government to bounce back have seen little social or economic impact. It is clear that the historical failure to develop the internal industries coupled with a brutal embargo on a country almost exclusively dependent on imports, damages the civilians the most in the long as well as the short term. These policies have brought Venezuela to a critical and appalling situation from which it is far from recovering.

Chapter V: Middle East

Amy Espinoza Caldas

Sykes-Picot Agreement (1917)

What happened? *The Sykes-Picot Agreement* (1916) was a treaty that recorded the partition of the Middle East, carried out in secret by Great Britain and France, with the support of Russia. This accord ignored the promises made to the Arabs in reward for their participation against the Ottoman Empire. Instead, it would divide Syria, Iraq, Lebanon and Palestine in areas under the control of British and French forces. It is named after the two main participants: Sir Mark Sykes, representing Great Britain, and François Georges-Picot, on behalf of France.

Why did it happen? In the ashes of World War I, Edward Lawrence, more commonly known as Laurence of Arabia, an agent of British Intelligence made a proposal to the leader of the Hashemites, King Hussein: if the Arabs joined in defeating the Ottomans, the Western powers would support and recognize the creation of an Arab Nation, a Great Arabia that would include Iraq, Jordan, Syria, Lebanon, Palestine, and the Arabian Peninsula. At first sight, it was a win-win situation since Europe knew they could not defeat Sultan Mehmet V on their own accord. Once the war was won and the Ottomans were crushed, the agreement with the Arabs followed. There would not be an Arab Nation, instead the British, the French and, in an even more sneaky manner, the Russians would have a free card to do what was best for their interests. If the people from the nations they were so treacherously dominating had ever a slice of hope for the future, they were in for a rude awakening. The future was not meant to be theirs.

Immediate consequences: To keep up the facade, the *Agreement* provided a framework that seemed to enable the possibility of an independent Arab nation. There can be no real independence whatsoever if the core of the *Agreement* sliced the Arab identity and made of its remaining pieces a broken puzzle that can never be put back together. A distribution of five zones was proposed. First, there would be a British control zone (zone B) and a French control zone (zone A). As it was foreseeable, those in control of these areas had the undisputed right to do as they pleased in terms of trade and businesses, and they had a veto upon who could be admitted as a representative of the Arab Confederation. A color-system was established to indicate the division on a map: blue for the French and red for the British. The French territory comprised the coast with the Mediterranean, from the heart of Anatolia to Palestine. The British area was composed of the former Mesopotamia all the way to the Persian Gulf. A gray zone would be under a scattered international control: Palestine, or what was the same, a land molded by global forces to be a vessel of murderous conflict.

Lennin's WikiLeaks & the Start of the Zino-Arab War: It is commonly said that God might forgive a sin if this has not raised a scandal, whether this is true or not, matters little for the impact this logic has held over how politics work. Starving for revenge after being left out of the loot by the British and French, Lenin did what we now call a Wikileaks-style move and spilled out all the details of the infamous *Agreement* to the newspapers *Izvestia* and *Pravda*. *The Manchester Guardian* followed and, soon, the news shattered any hope that was left for the Arabs, by bringing the realization that they were not citizens. They were not even conquered; they had been turned into puppets in the midst of a fire out of their control. In 1917 that fire was enlarged when the UK's Foreign Secretary Arthur Balfour declared that the time for a Zionist or Jewish nation had arrived, and that he had found the perfect parchment to write its foundations: Palestine. Once again, what the Arabs wanted did not matter.

What can we learn from it? Life is constructed upon so many realities that it is hard to fathom a society, let alone a nation, where the abundant flow of differences do not collide with the individualism of each culture. The idea of building an Arab Nation covering all the richness of the Middle East and beyond had little to none rate of succeeding. But what about preserving identities without the ashes of a perennial conflict? A series of letters written between countries that should not have been involved at all, prevented the world from seeing a Middle East outside a poorly fabricated reality.

The Balfour Declaration (1917)

What happened? Every story has an origin, a point where everything changes for good. For the disaster that shocked Palestine and the Middle East and saw the birth of Israel, that point is known as the *Balfour Declaration*. Issued on November 1, 1917, amidst World War I, Foreign Secretary of the British Empire, Lord Arthur Balfour voiced publicly the interest of his nation to promote the installation of a national Jewish state in Palestine. The declaration took form in a letter sent to Lionel Walter Rothschild, a leader of the Zionist community. Palestine was under the occupation of the UK and Jews only represented 10% of its population.

Why did it happen? Basically, the *Balfour Declaration* not only altered the landscape of a country, but it radically shifted the destiny of a whole population. The word 'controversial' is often used to discuss why something that radical had to happen at all. It has been hinted by some that the British government had a close bond with the Zionists and so Lord Balfour did this out of friendship. Geopolitically speaking, however, there is the hypothesis that the British government was more interested in controlling Palestine than making the Jews happy. Palestine with its borders to the Suez Canal and Egypt was in a privileged position that Britain was not ready to relinquish. And of course, it was a matter of looking good in front of the Jewish community in the United States and Russia, fundamental partners to win World War I.

France's hidden role: It is customary to link the *Balfour Declaration* to the self-interests of the UK. But such a decision could not come to be, if not for the support of some allies. As reported per Al-Jazeera, in 1917, Jules Cambon, a French diplomat, sent a letter to Nahum Sokolow, a well-known Polish figure in the Zionist movement, in which he expressed the French government's support of the Jewish colonization of Palestine.

How did the Arab community respond? By request of the US President Woodrow Wilson, in 1919 a commission was formed to research how the Arabs and more precisely Palestinians felt with regard to having their land moved as if it were a puzzle of foreign interests. No surprises here, for the Palestinians the *Balfour Declaration* was the worst kind of imaginable offense. Not only was their home being offered to a minority, but it was also a decision in which they had no say whatsoever.

What can we learn from it? Later on, in this very section, the significance and impact that the *Balfour Declaration* had and still has upon how Palestinians are viewed will be further reviewed. For now, let's focus on understanding what this decision really meant. A foreign power acted without any legal ground over the fate of an oppressed nation. What the British government and its allies did, went beyond creating a nation for the Jews, instead, they literally granted Israel the immunity to proceed with an ethnic cleansing.

Turkish War of Independence (1919-1923)

What happened? In a post-World War I Ottoman society where defeat and long-dated resentment towards the commercial influence of the Western Powers, the Turks were exhausted and saw the power of the Sultan as something thoroughly extinguished by the consequences of said war. International troops occupied Istanbul and some coastal areas of Anatolia. In addition, very harsh conditions were imposed via the peace treaty after the war and most of their territories were distributed among the victorious powers, especially in favor of France and Great Britain. To worsen things, in 1919, Greece invaded some regions of Turkey (Edirne, Bursa and İzmir) thanks to the support of the Supreme Allied War Council. As a reaction, the Turkish National Movement was created and led by Kemal Atatürk, a distinguished commander. This military and nationalist movement soon acquired such strength that, although Turkey had been defeated, terms were set that were convenient to the interest and well-being of the nation. The members of the National Movement went against occupation and rejected the partition contained in the Treaty of Sèvres. Once the war was over this Treaty was replaced by the Treaty of Kars (October 1921) and Lausanne (1923). By virtue of the latter, the Allies were obligated to leave Anatolia and the Eastern Thrace. The Republic of Turkey was officially founded on October 29th, 1923, with the election of its first president, Kemal Atatürk. However, the Turkish War of Independence left an abundance of civil casualties, including the deaths of 264,000 Greeks, between 60,000 and 250,000 Armenians and 15,000 Turks.

Background: When the Armistice of Mudros was signed in 1918, the Ottoman Empire and the Allies of World War I aimed at, at least in theory, terminating the armed conflict in the Middle East, the stage of the War. By agreement, the Allies were allowed to control the Straits of the Dardanelles and the Bosphorus. In return, it was announced that the Allies had no intention whatsoever to bring the Empire down, but, as the Sykes-Picot scheme demonstrates, this was not the case. Dismantling the Ottoman Empire was always the main goal behind the Allies' actions. On November 13, 1918, the Allies showed their true colors when they sent a French brigade to claim Constantinople (Istanbul). This was the first of many invasions to come. In between the chaos, the Greeks recognized the opportunity to make their presence a tool for more in-deep invasion. Their next move was to expand their occupation to Anatolia.

Turkish National Movement: Heroes are usually born from a traditional recipe: a cup of reality, half a cup of myth and a tone of almost magical willpower. Commander Mustafa Kemal Atakürk witnessed how the glory of the Bosphorus was constrained by the weight of foreign flags controlling the winds of what was meant to be a land of freedom. He vowed to do anything within his grasp to defeat them. But heroic actions do not belong to a single name, they are the result of a collective identity, thus, in Anatolia, Turks were forming associations and strategies to defend what belonged to them. What started as a local dispute, mainly, against non-local Muslims rapidly became a threat for the occupying powers. Trying to contain the fire before it started, the Allies asked the Sultan to impose order. By recommendation of the Grand vizier, the Sultan assured them that order would come at the hands of Mustafa Kemal, a respected and loyal officer. Nevertheless, the dawn of May 19, 1919, would carry a different spectacle: Mustafa Kemal landed on Samsun, and instead showed loyalty to the Turkish.

He arrived to fight for the salvation of his people, and for the birth of a country. The political and armed activities that followed are known as the core of the Turkish National Movement.

War & Consequences: With the increasing support of the national forces, the Turkish National Movement quickly became a road to create a Grand National Assembly. Since its headquarters were in Ankara, the call for a war of independence was made official. Kemal's power relied on Kemalism, an ideology that had as its main principles the creation of a republic, the establishment of a secular administration and the presence of nationalism with a mixed economy.

The Turkish War of Independence was fought between the followers of Kemal and the Allies and their helpers: France and the United Kingdom on the Southern front, Italy in Constantinople, Greece on the Western front and Armenia on the Eastern. Despite the fact that the conflict extended throughout all fronts, Turkey's fate was not decided until the Greco-Turkish War. As the Greek army made advancements to the Sakarya River, a close location to the base of the Grand National Assembly, Mustafa Kemal took the leadership of the Assembly's forces and led the Battle of Sakarya (August 23-September 13, 1921) where the Greeks were overpowered and defeated. Yet, the war continued when the Allies, underestimating Kemal's influence, attempted to sign a new Treaty of Sevres, only to be rejected. A year later in August 1922, constant attacks ravaged the Greek lines in the

Battle of Dumlupınar and Turkish forces regained control of Smyrna on September 9, 1922. Kemal wrote to the League of Nations that the Turks could not be contained, and any disgrace that happened afterwards would not be his responsibility. Exactly nine days after that, on September 18, the foreign armies were forced to leave. On November 1 of that very year the Turkish Parliament abolished the Sultanate and a republic was built.

What can we learn from it? Wars are messes that rarely, if ever, result in anything else aside from raw weakness and malice. It becomes extremely troublesome to determine winners and losers when so much has been lost. The Turkish Independence War is a special case, as it was not just a reaction against oppression, it led to the creation of a nation. The Ottoman Empire's loss during World War I precipitated the invasion of Constantinople, yet, the Turkish nation and the Istanbul we know today fought for and attained an unparalleled and untamable liberty.

Syrian Revolt (1925-1927)

What happened? The Syrian Revolt, also known as the Great Druze Revolt (1925-1927) was a failed attempt on the Syrian's behalf to get rid of French control, that had been imposed as yet another consequence of the shameful Sykes-Picot Agreement. A lack of systematization among the differing factions (Sunni, Druze, Alawite, Christians and Shias) was among the reasons for the failure.

Context: Once the Ottoman Empire was defeated, losing its presence over the Arab landscape, the Allies took hold of the territories. Britain claimed Palestine, Transjordan and Iraq, and France was adjudicated with Syria. Naturally, this maneuver was not welcomed by the majority of the Syrian population and only non-Muslims factions seemed to be content with the change, however, this satisfaction was marred by the

French decision of dividing the country into a series of administrative regions, increasing local discomfort and segregation.

Causes: In addition to the governmental chaos, Syrians also had to witness how the local upper class, traditionally in charge of the state affairs, was bluntly left aside as the French started to administrate the communities disregarding the inner processes of the previous system. On the outskirts of the city, life was not any brighter, and Tribesmen who had to endure trade taxes and bans were eager to stand up against the oppression. Nonetheless, if a sole reason for the Revolt had to be pinpointed behind the Revolt, it would come from the hands of the Druze population.

The Druze region was under the control of a group of nobles known as the Majlis who had expected to strike a deal with the French, similar to the one established under Ottoman rule. According to tradition, the al-Atrash family was the one that should hold power over the Druze area. However, in 1923, Selim al-Atrash stepped down from said responsibility and the Majlis replaced him with French Officer Captain Cabrillet. This communicated the notion that being in agreement with France was being in agreement with oppression. Shortly after, Selim al-Atrash was arrested and this was followed by civil unrest.

Revolt & Consequences: On August 23, 1925, the Sultan Pasha al-Atrash officially announced the revolution against the French, which gathered public support across the country. The beginning of the revolution looked promising following the Syrian victory in both the Battle of al-Kafr and the Battle of al- Mazraa. Subsequently, France called troops from Morocco and Senegal, outnumbering the Syrians in soldiers and surpassing them in weapon technology. As a result, the flames for a change gave their last breath in 1927, Sultan al-Atrash was sentenced to death and fled to TransJordan. Ten years later al-Atrash was welcomed back as a hero, following the guidelines of the Treaty of Syrian Independence.

What can we learn from it? In spite of not having obtained the ultimate goal, the Great Syrian Revolt is seen as a stepping stone towards independence and as a national holiday in the country. The reason? Victories are not just restricted to momentary lapses, and the greatest come in the shape of small steps walking in cohesion to achieve something that for many is totally unreachable.

Saudi-Yemeni War (1934)

What happened? The beginning of the conflict transpired in March 1934, when King Ibn Saud ordered the Crown Prince of Saudi Arabia (later King Saud) to reoccupy the municipalities in the Tehama Highlands that the Imam of Yemen had taken over (Victors in Yemen 1934, 7). According to *The Argus*, it was in Ibn Saud's interest to cease the disputes with the Iman by using diplomatic methods, but this proved impossible to accomplish considering the latter's repeatedly aggressive attitude (22 Mar. 1934, 21). There was no option but war. On March 20, 1934, Saudi Arabia declared war on Yemen. Since the Saudis were better prepared and trained they defeated Yemen in May of the same year. *The Treaty of Taif* was signed by both parties, and it stated that the Saudis would keep control over the tribal frontiers. While such a short conflict might have appeared irrelevant at that moment, the years to come would demonstrate that, in some cases, having signed a treaty is not a guarantee of peace.

Context: With the flames of the Great War extinguished and the system of the Ottomans almost forgotten, King Ibn Saud controlled pretty much the entire area of Arabia, except for Yemen and some smaller states like Oman, Kuwait and Bahrain. Yet, some tribal regions remained undivided due to their reputation of being difficult to handle, even for the Ottomans. Embodying a forbidden and tempting fruit, these regions would become the reason behind the war.

How did it happen? History knows well that there have been many wars that did not start by direct confrontation but rather by proxies and indirect relations. This is exactly the case of the Yemen-Saudi War when Idrissi, the Emir of Asir, an independent region between Saudi Arabia and Yemen, granted the presence of the Saudis as a means to keep his power. Little did Emir Idrissi know that by doing so, the Saudis would grasp the opportunity to expand their territories all over his land. Faced with the unexpected, he betrayed his loyalty and fled to Yemen in order to obtain the support of the Yemeni King, Iman Yahya. With the purpose of maintaining all the routes of dialogue open, King Saud sent a delegation led by his own son. As a response, Iman Yahya jailed the prince and ordered the army to mobilize towards Saudi lands.

Development and Treaty of Taif: Seven weeks of conflict were enough to paint a landscape of defeat for the Yemeni army. The amount and quality of their munition proved insufficient in contrast to the modern deployment of weapons of the Saudis. Even when relying on Turkey's support, Yemen had to witness how King Saud's power conquered, not only the disputed lands, but it also reached the coast of Yemen. Making concessions was the only way out of the mayhem that, by that point, was creating discomfort within Yemen's population. The Treaty of Taif was drafted on May 12, 1934, and while it brought relief to both Saudis and Yemenis it was meant to be short-lived as the Treaty itself established that peace would only last twenty years.

What can we learn from it? At first glance this conflict can be studied as yet another geographical dispute, but a deeper analysis indicates the main point of discrepancy between the Yemenis and the Saudis was their identity. Or at least in the perception they had about themselves. For the orthodox Westernized view of the word "Arab", deserts and camels are a must. For Yemen, back in the day, this portrait was an offense to the real Arab identity, as the nomadic lifestyle of the dunes was considered only fitting for barbarians.

Middle East & World War II: A Summary (1939-1945)

What happened? In 1941, as the world looked on in shock at the Pearl Harbor attack, the Middle East, a region shaped by lies and obscure intrigues, felt the poison of World War II knocking down its doors with the force of a sandstorm. Little is said about the stage ignited by the Second World War in the Middle East, but just because something is unnoticed does not mean there is no story worthy of having its own voice.

In 1941, for instance, many were contemplating how to gain control of Iran. As one of the few independent nations of the region—let's remember how fragmented the Middle East was due to the intrusion of foreign powers (i.e. *Sykes-Picot Agreement*). The Kingdom of Iran feared that the proximity of a war, involving Britain and a torn France, could pose a threat to its sovereignty. Suddenly, Germany's Nazis and Italy's Fascists were welcomed as possible allies in maintaining and, perhaps, even recovering the Middle East's stolen independence.

Libya: As a consequence of the Great War, by World War II the country was breathing under Italy's boots. This was not a voluntary choice, because in 1915 and the years that followed the nation had learned that rising against Italy was guaranteed to unleash atrocities across its population. When Benito Mussolini rose to power, Libya became a colony of Italy. Fighting against such imposed fate was not a possibility.

Egypt: The tormented relationship this country had with Great Britain was the beginning of another wreckage. In 1936, King Faruk I signed the Anglo-Egyptian Treaty of Friendship and Collaboration with England, which represented the opening of a pompous and dubious path for the British Army to once again occupy Egypt. The creation of the Muslim Brotherhood was a nationalist response to the King's actions. Tired of the abuse brought by colonialism and in search of implementing pan-Arabism (ideology that advocated for the unification of all Arab communities), Egypt was transformed into the perfect nest for the surge of the Egyptian National Socialist Party. Deeply socialist and with greetings similar to that of the Nazis, it is no wonder people like General Aziz Ali Al-Masri, Chief of the Egyptian Army General Staff worked for Admiral Wilhelm Canaris, a prominent member of the German Intelligence. When the War broke out, the association between Egypt and the Third Reich was a well-known secret.

Saudi Arabia: A young nation—it came to be in 1916 once the Ottomans were defeated— was not ready to be at the mercy of ravenous global players. Its geographical location and the oil under its soil was a jewel coveted by many. With those concerns in mind in 1936, the royal family opted to befriend Italy by accepting the Italian annexation of Ethiopia. In response, Mussolini expressed his gratitude by offering advisers, weapons and aircraft, the foundation of the Saudi Air Force. With the collaboration of Iraq's German Ambassador, German soldiers were accepted as instructors of the Saudi Army.

Yemen: The closeness of the British Army was again the catalyst for the local government to seek support within the arms of Mussolini. In 1937, right after the British installed its forces close to the Yemeni border, the country followed a similar path to the one chosen by the Saudis and asked the Italians for military training.

Syria: Overpowered by the French and with crushed hopes after the failure of the Great Syrian Revolt, the spirits of the country in the age of the Second World War were anxious for a change. Secessionists movements like the National Bloc and the Syrian-Palestine Council flowed naturally. In 1937 this nationalism erupted into the confection of the National Socialist Syrian Party, a clear copycat of the Third Reich's ideology.

Iraq: In 1933, British Intelligence forces discovered Iraq was selling arms to the Syrian rebels who fought against France. This, however, was not random but a carefully planned strategy approved by Iraqi Prime Minister Yassin Paschá Al-Haschimi. The shipment was captured, and the warning was dire: Britain could invade Iraq at any moment. In reaction, King Gazi I decided to strengthen the relationship of his country with Germany. While this worked for a couple of years, King Gazi died in a dubious car accident just a year before World War II was declared. Their relations formally broken, Great Britain and Iraq stood blatantly on rival sides.

Iraq & the Allies, An Unexpected Alliance and Iran's role: In 1941 a coup d'état was launched by Iraqi nationalists. Back in Britain, the precarious position of France and its inclination towards Hitler was a reason for concern, due to the fact that their power in the Middle East could then be challenged by both France and Germany. Once the coup established a government under the hands of Rashid Ali, Great Britain tenaciously attacked Iraq, to the extent that the new ruler was forced to leave his country and hide in Germany.

To obliterate any traces of animosity, Britain's army invaded all the provinces that had shown support for Ali's government, and promised that once the War finished, Iraq would be fully independent. Months later, in June, the URSS proceeded to occupy Iraq, precipitating the unpredictable: Iraq was propelled to be part of the Allies. In need of British and American supplies, it was imperative to find the safest route: Iran's roads. King Reza Shah was clear in his refusal to allow it. Shortly after, he was forced to change his mind when both Soviets and British launched an offensive that crushed all of Iran's defenses. King Sha was also compelled into exile. The Middle

East would refrain from any revolt, as a reward, many countries would finally obtain their liberty.

What can we learn from it? If something can be learned from this historical chapter is that in some occasions, you can still have an influence on how the plot develops even when you are not the lead actor. History would have declared a different World War II victor if not for the Middle East and its capabilities for communication as well as the constant provision of fuel for the Allies' army across all fronts.

Arab-Israeli War (1948)

What happened? One of the most fascinating aspects of history is that nothing is completely written without having heard multiple perspectives. May 14, 1948, is a date when a single occurrence developed and yet has two very opposing meanings. In Israel, it is a reason for celebration, since it represents the establishment of the first Israeli country. In Palestine, however, the memory of that day is met with sorrow, as it is a bitter souvenir of the day when over 700,000 Palestinians were obliged to leave their country. Why? To answer this, one must turn their attention to the 1917 Balfour Declaration which contains the UK's scandalous promise to the Jews: their holy land was waiting for them in Palestine. If the Jews were ever to have a country, it would be in Palestine.

Why did it happen? When the fire of World War II ceased, and it was understood that the wounds carried by the Jews had the size of a genocide, there was no possible delay for the Balfour Declaration. A humanitarian crisis was unleashed when hundreds of Jews decided to forge a new fate by crossing the Mediterranean with the hope of finding a place to call home. But the sight of their ships was rejected by every country that saw them coming near to its shores. Even the British sent them back to France when they tried to reach Haifa Port.

Determined not to give up, the Jews refused to go ashore and went into a hunger strike for three weeks. A crisis was in the making. By the time the ships were destined to return to Germany, media across the world turned the crisis into a humanitarian disaster.

In 1948 the flag of the State of Israel was seen, for the first time, waving in the United Nations' building in New York. A decision had been reached: the area of Palestine occupied by the British since the fall of the Ottoman Empire would be, from that day on, the State of Israel. The Jews broke out in joy, while the Palestinians were nothing but outraged, a day later nothing but a mandate dictated they had to leave their homes. Ben Gurion, Father of Israel and its first Prime Minister, was well into conquering a Holy Land. How much "holiness" can be involved in a war is still open to debate.

More than seventy years later, the conflict is far from being resolved.

War & Development: The Arab League, formed in 1945 and composed of Algeria, Egypt, Saudi Arabia, Iraq, Jordan, Yemen, Syria, and Libya, saw the birth of the State of Israel as a death sentence for the Arab people. Naturally, war was declared. Egypt, Syria, Jordan and Iraq launched an attack against the newcomers. Had that war involved only Jews against Arabs, perhaps the precarious early condition of the Israeli militia could have favored the advance of the League. Nevertheless, with the support of the US the cards of good fortune were turned towards Israel. The constant intervention of international diplomacy was the reason behind many cease-fires during the one year that the war lasted, granting Israel sufficient room to maneuver and even more endorsement.

Consequences: In March 1949, hostilities *officially* ceased, and Israel signed armistices with Egypt, Syria, Lebanon and Transjordan. It was agreed that Israel would maintain control over three-fourths of what was formerly known as the Mandate of Palestine and a quarter more of what was first allocated by the United Nations partition plan.

Notwithstanding, the war was far from concluding and the years that followed were the stage of the Suez Crisis of 1956, the Six-Day War of 1967, the Ramadan or Yom Kippur War of 1973, the Lebanon War of 1982 and, certainly, the Palestinian Intifadas.

What can we learn from it? Wars raise a different kind of dust, no matter how much you clean, the dirty cloudiness remains, which makes it impossible to pick a side without ending up morally compromised. While it would be simpler to describe the conflict between Palestine and Israel as a dispute of faiths, the past seventy years have repeatedly depicted a puzzle where the biggest piece has always been moved by political interests. Jerusalem is still claimed by both nations as the capital of their beliefs. Regrettably, geopolitical convenience has dictated that the party's voice that can provide the greatest benefit is the one that must be heard. Although Western control in the Middle East halted decades ago, the weight of its selfishness is yet to disappear.

Kurdish-Turkish Conflict (1978-Present)

The Kurds through facts:
- They have lived in the Middle East for over 2000 years
- They rise up to around 30 million people dispersed among Iraq, Syria, Iran and Turkey.
- Their ultimate goal is to have an independent nation, something they have never had.
- In Turkey, they are the biggest minority: 18 million people.

What happened with Turkey? In 1978, amidst Turkish violence against the Kurds, Abdullah Öcalan founded the Kurdish Workers Party (PKK), which fought to gain recognition as the official representative of the yet-to-be-built, Kurdish State. Starting in 1984 this armed force has been fighting directly against Turkey for the right to have a Kurdish nation. The estimated count of fatal losses for this ongoing conflict is nearly 40,000.

Why is this happening? To answer this question, we must go back to the empire of the Medes in the BC era. It is said that the Kurds came from the Medes, ancient inhabitants of the area now known as Iran. Once the empire fell, the Kurds settled for a tribal society, with some similarities to the feudal structure of the Middle Ages. Problems arose during the Ottoman expansion when they fell into a partition of influences: one still molded by Iran, the other inclined to the control of the Turks. Complications were only beginning when a shift in power and international agreements (namely, *Treaty of Sevres*, *Treaty of Lausanne*, and the infamous *Sykes-Picot Agreement*) moved the scale of supremacy to the likes of Western countries. Correspondingly, frontiers were crafted with a strategic mindset and the Kurds were left to wander in between. Turkey never acknowledged their existence, and they were subjected to constant discrimination and a military witch-hunt. These circumstances pushed the country-less population to the southern part of Turkey, the area along the north of Syria, Iraq and Iran is called Kurdistan. In 1984 when the Kurds started to answer with gunpowder to the inequity promoted by the Turkish government, the PKK was declared a terrorist group: their leaders were hunted and their militia, the Unities of Popular Protection (YPG), was equally persecuted.

International response: Alliances are the base for diplomacy, interests are the ground where realpolitik grows. World powers such as the United States and the European Union have also deemed the PKK as a terrorist organization, a terrorist organization that has been a quintessential part of the occidental fight against ISIS. With a privileged position in the mountains of Syria, the Kurds have battled shoulder to shoulder with European and American soldiers to stop the spread of ISIS. This unspoken alliance came to pieces with Trump's decision of withdrawing American forces from the ground, leaving the Kurds in the awkward position of having to make a pact with Bashar al-Assad's ruthless government in order to keep the battle against ISIS and survive a renewed series of Turkish attacks.

What can we learn from it? The Kurds might feel that their aspirations have no importance whatsoever for the international community since their demand for a Kurdish country is one that has been repeatedly ignored. Withal, there is no denying that the decision of the United States to no longer consider them necessary, allures other global forces to show an interest. Russia, that has always been interested in surpassing the US, has already stepped up to demand Turkey for a cease of attacks against the Kurdish population. A culture, a language, a society, an influential army: Kurdistan has all the components of a nation, it is the rest of the world that has a problem perceiving it as such.

The Iranian Revolution (1979)

By Armita Hosseini (Collaborator)

What happened? The 1979 Iranian Revolution, also known as the Islamic Revolution, sought to rid the country of the Pahlavi dynasty. This dynasty had only two kings, with the first being Reza Shah, and the second Mohammad Reza Shah, who became the leader of Iran after his father's abdication during World War II. The initial demonstrations began on January 7, 1978, after an Iranian newspaper published an article that was critical of Ayatollah Ruhollah Khomeini, who was living in Paris at the time. At first, the demonstrations were quite small, yet after armed forces fired during the demonstration killing some protesters, the protests began to grow. Although the 1979 Revolution resulted in the establishment of the Islamic Republic of Iran, it is important to note that the protest's original aim was not to create an Islamic state. Instead, it started as a typical uprising of dissatisfied citizens who wanted to overthrow a government they believed to be inadequate and unable to meet their needs, including:

economic inequality, political repression, and a corrupt regime. Mohammad Reza Shah did not understand why there were demonstrations against him, and thought that the protesters were communists supported by the British. Eventually, on January 16, 1979, he left Iran. Following his leave, the Islamic Republic of Iran was created based on Khomeini's idea of what an Islamic Republic should be. This meant the establishment of Velayat-e-faqih.

The demonstrations: After the newspaper article was published on January 7, 1978, thousands of students from religious school and Iranian youth—many of which were unemployed immigrants from the countryside—began protesting. During these protests, many people were killed by the officers, which further fueled the citizens' aggression and desire to continue demonstrating. In Shi'i tradition, which is a branch of Islam, it is custom to commemorate the forty-day milestone of mourning; therefore, forty days following the killing of the protesters, further demonstrations were carried out in Iran. During these protests, more people continued to be killed, which only increased the intensity of demonstrations to come. In the month of October, oil workers went on strike, which put a stop to the oil industry. Subsequently, on December 10, people from across the country began to protest, with hundreds of thousands protesting in the capital city of Tehran alone.

Black Friday Massacre: On September 8, 1978, Mohammad Reza Shah imposed martial law; yet Iranian citizens did not obey his orders and took to the streets where they carried out further demonstrations. Protesters gathered at Jaleh Square in Tehran, to express their distaste for the Pahlavi Dynasty. This day was important as it resulted in many people getting shot, ending any hope for compromise between the Shah and the citizens. It was the beginning of the end of the Pahlavi Dynasty in Iran, which was a pivotal moment in determining the future of Iran and the Middle East. The Jaleh Square was renamed to the Square of Martyrs, and after the Iranian Revolution, Khomeini created the Martyrs Foundation to record the name of all the people who were "martyred" by the Shah's regime. However, later research found that the number of killings was likely exaggerated by Khomeini, and the real number was very similar to that published by the Shah's government. Yet, due to the Shah's great loss of legitimacy, people were no longer willing to believe information provided by their government.

Aftermath: Shah's leave and the establishment of the Islamic Republic of Iran: On January 16, 1978, Shah and his family fled Iran in what was described as a "vacation". Following this, over a million people took to demonstrating in Tehran and provided wide appeal to Khomeini, who arrived in Iran on February 1, 1979. On February 11, the Iranian armed forces declared neutrality, which permanently drove out the Shah's government. Following widespread support in a public referendum on April 1, 1979, Khomeini declared an Islamic Republic of Iran. All left-wing, nationalist, and intellectual allies were excluded from the new regime. In the same fashion, the Family Protection Act of 1967, which provided additional rights to women in marriage and was significantly amended in 1975, was declared void. Mosque-based revolutionary bands known as komītehs (committees) marched in the streets, enforcing strict Islamic dress codes and behavior. The violence was often greater than that under the Shah. There was much anti-Western sentiment by the government, followed by brutality and persecution.

Velayat-e-faqih (Governance of the Jurist): The Assembly of Experts (Majles-e Khobregān) put forth a referendum, which was widely supported, and resulted in the establishment of Velayat-e-faqih based on Khomeini's vision of what an Islamic government should be. This gave the greatest power to the rahbar (leader). A sharia law scholar would ultimately have authority, because he was more knowledgeable than anyone on law and justice. While there would be a legislature, prime minister, and president, their decisions could all be overturned by the supreme ruler (rahbar), who, from 1979 until his death in 1989, was Khomeini.

What can we learn from it? The Iranian Revolution was a turning point in determining life in the Middle East, as well as Iran's international relations. It started as an uprising by dissatisfied citizens, not as an attempt to establish an Islamic state. Looking back on this event, a lesson that can be learned is how the shortcomings of a current ruler or state of affairs can be extrapolated by others to move forward their own agendas. The Iranian citizens enthusiastically and willingly welcomed Khomeini and his ideals because they were unhappy with the status quo and hoped for a better future. Many protested in the streets with the desire to contribute to making a positive change. Yet in the present day, the majority of Iranian citizens tend to agree that the government that was established was far from what people desired or imagined at first. It has been over four decades since the Iranian Revolution and, to this day, Iran has been managed according to the ideals Khomeini set forth in 1979.

First Palestinian Intifada (1987)

What happened? The word 'intifada' means uprising in Arabic, and in the context of Palestinian history it tells the story of two protests against Israel, the first in 1987 and the second in 2000. For this chapter, the former will be addressed. In 1987 Palestinians gathered their voices and courage to speak up about the constant discrimination and violence at the hands of Israel. It started with civil disobedience (general strikes and boycotts) and it led to some violent acts such as the launching of rocks and Molotov cocktails against the Israelis.

Why did it happen? Generally, the main reason for the Intifada is linked to the murder of four Palestinian workers by Israeli forces. On December 8, 1987, a military convoy hit a civilian car, instantly killing the four Palestinians in a refugee camp in the Gaza Strip. While this was the flame that ignited the eruption of public outrage, the fire had been long provoked by the hardships Palestinians suffered including poverty, high rates of unemployment, and oppression.

How did it evolve? Enraged, the Palestinian youth took the streets, treating them as a canvas to portray their utter discontent about how their people were treated. They stopped attending work, they refused to acquire anything that came from Israel, they stopped paying taxes, and barricades were displayed. It was meant to be a civilian movement, but Israel had other intentions "which included a government policy of breaking the bones of protestors" (PBS 2019). The Israeli Information Centre for Human Rights' reports indicate that a 1,000 Palestinians were killed and thousands were imprisoned.

Peace talks: It was in 1991 when peace talks became a viable option thanks to the US's intervention. Yet, the cease of violence did not occur until 1993, with the signing of the *Oslo Accords* between Palestine and Israel which stated ceasefire for a period of five years.

What can we learn from it? As it will be evident later on in this section, the *Oslo Accords* provided little room for the Palestinians to make their claims valid. The conditions that have devastated their society for so long have not disappeared, if anything, they have gotten worse. The backbone of the Intifadas is still in the hearts of every person who stands up against human rights abuse.

The Gulf War (1991)

What happened? The Gulf War, aka the Operation Desert Storm. The calendar marked a date: January 16, 1991, the protagonist was US President George H. W Bush, as for the story it was drafted in an announcement of a military operation against Iraq. Months before, Iraq had forcefully occupied Kuwait. As a response, an international coalition of thirty-five countries, led by the US, was formed under

United Nations Security Council Resolution 678, causing the deployment of more than 900,000 troops across the Saudi-Iraq region. Once the United Nation's deadline for leaving Kuwait was ignored by the Iraqi government—under Saddam Hussein's leadership—the coalition went into full attack mode, bombarding from air and sea. In February, they staged an operation in the ground coming dangerously close to the center of Iraq, pressuring Hussein to both abandon his expansionists dreams and walk away from Kuwait. Casualties showed a raw disparity. The coalition lost hundreds of lives… Iraqi losses climbed up to the tens of thousands.

Why did it happen? Kuwait, a fully independent yet small state, known for its colossal oil reserves was invaded on August, 2, 1990, under the command of Saddam Hussein. Iraq was not a stranger to the power of oil, but there were disputes about the ownership of the reserves located on the border between the two countries. Kuwait was quickly outnumbered and occupied, its institutions claimed and a new government installed. The United Nations condemned the attack and imposed economic sanctions with the intention of stopping the invasion, to no effect.

The United States, on the other hand, was already on its way to send troops to Saudi Arabia. The eagerness of this country did not come from a humanitarian spirit, but from the anxiety to lose their influence over an area that had such steep amounts of oil.

How did it happen? No nation, since the days of World War I, had ever seen a military formation so imposing: almost a million soldiers from the coalition and half a million from Iraq were supported by thousands of tanks and aircraft. Not a day or night went by when the coalition was not bombarding key strongholds of the Iraqi army in Iraq and Kuwait.

By February 28, Iraq was keen to withdraw its troops from Kuwait, but they were not willing to leave without a final strike and, on their way out, Iraqi soldiers burned hundreds of oil wells, so they could never be used again.

Consequences: Inequity is an accurate concept to describe the outcome of this war, while it remains true that the coalition suffered losses, the Iraqi death toll is still unconfirmed. The infrastructure of the country was left in ashes: official buildings, roads, public areas... All devastated. The Iraqi people were not in better conditions, with the weight of the economic sanctions crushing them, their development was abruptly interrupted. It still is.

What can we learn from it? The coalition's success was measured by the defeat of Iraq's invasion of Kuwait, but leaving Saddam Hussein in power, even after all these years, brings questions about how effective that decision was if his repressive government and his link to weapons of mass destruction was allegedly the reason behind the US return to the country in 2003.

The Oslo Accords (1993/1995)

What happened? Even being someone's enemy requires a balance between the parties, there has to be some level of recognition. This is what happened with Israel and Palestine—more precisely, with the Palestine Liberation Organization (PLO)—that officially acknowledged the existence of the other. Signed around 1993 and 1995 in the White House, the accords were named after the city where the secret conversations occurred.

The story: In 1979, PLO's Chairman Yasser Arafat, considered neutral Norway as a suitable place for opening a line of communication with Israel. In spite of that, Israel was not interested.

Ten years forward, in the context of the Palestinian Intifada, Arafat had to accept UN Resolutions 242 and 338 granting Israel "a secure and recognized boundaries" (UNdocs, 22 Nov. 1967, 8) and a free pass to keep the occupation over specific areas of the West Bank. Additionally, Israel was facing international backlash for its savage response against the Palestinian protesters. If there was ever a time to start a dialogue, it was now. Curiously enough, Norway was not altogether neutral, because out of 157 members of Parliament, 87 belonged to the group 'Friends of Israel'.

How was it developed? After the Gulf War, Palestine was in a weakened position, the PLO had backed Iraq and Saddam Hussein in 1991, awakening the wrath of other Arab and Western powers. This was by no means a favorable start. This was made evident when important topics were excluded from Israel's conversations such as: the matter of illegal settlements in the occupied West Bank and Gaza Strip, the status of Jerusalem, and any other related subjects to security and borders.

Instead, the *Oslo Accords* focused on setting up a plausible framework for a better governance of the invaded areas and, if possible, further negotiations. Meant to last only five years, truth is, peace was never attained. The only thing these agreements accomplished was to put the internal administration of major Palestinian cities and areas of the occupied West Bank and Gaza Strip under the recently formed Palestinian Authority.

The Second Oslo Agreement, signed in 1995, divided the West Bank into three regions: Areas A, B and C. Area A was first designed to represent a 3% of the West Bank, but by 1999 this grew to 18%. Area B encompasses 21% of the region. The limits of the PA government are restricted to education, health and the economy, while the Israelis have absolute control of security and so-called justice. In a few words: Israel is free to detain and execute how they please. Area C can be used to measure the failure of the Oslo Accords, according to the conversations, this Area—representing 60% of the West Bank population—would be under the government of the PA. This is yet another fictitious tale, as Israel is still in control of it.

Norway's role: Norway's participation was no accident, in 1979, and in the days of the Iranian Revolution, the United States asked Norway to supply oil to Israel, in the light of the suspension of the Iranian supply. Norway set one condition before accepting: first, it was necessary to discuss it with Yasir Arafat. This was a calculated move on Norway's part, because, as it turned out, it had over a thousand soldiers in a reconnaissance mission in the Lebanese Civil War. PLO's fighters were involved and Norway was afraid of retaliation. Instead of opposing, Arafat saw it as an opportunity to pave the way to negotiate with Israel.

What can we learn from it? When Israeli PM Isaac Rabin and Arafat shook hands on the *Oslo Accords* in front of the White House, the United States presented it as a milestone for peace in the Middle East. More than twenty-five years later, it is crystal clear that what the US was presenting was fictitious. From the Israelites' perspective, the agreements should have never been signed with Arafat at the head of the Palestine government; many saw the PLO as a terrorist organization. For the Palestinians, even as they hoped for peace, the reality was dire. Israel's control would not cease. Not then, not now.

Second Palestinian Intifada (2000-2008)

What happened? Contrary to what was seen in the First Intifada, this one was marked with a heavier display of violence. This was mainly due to the broken negotiations between the Israeli Prime Minister Ehud Barak and the representative of the PLO (Palestine Liberation Organization) Yasser Arafat, as well as the fact that the then soon-to-be Israeli Prime Minister Ariel Sharon visited the Al-Aqsa Mosque, one of the most sacred places for the Islamic faith. Naturally, this was seen as a great provocation. As a result of the conflict, 1,000 Israelis and 3,000 Palestinians were killed.

Why did it happen? A day after Sharon's visit, Palestinians protested by launching stones at the Israelis who were in the Wailing Wall. The intervention of the Israel military forces ended with the murder of seven young Palestinians.

Context: To understand this, it is necessary to go back to the First Intifada and remember how disappointing the outcome of the *Oslo Accords* was for the Palestinians. The hope for change and autonomy was destroyed. The death of those young Palestinians was a dreadful event, but it was not the only horror Palestine had to face under the control of Israel. As a result, the streets of Gaza, Jordan and even Jerusalem filled up with anger, and it became impossible to keep the status quo any longer.

Why did it last so long? Another difference in relation to the First Intifada, aside from the violence, is that in Palestine a coalition was formed between the ordinary population and the politicians, between nationalists and Islamists. Their guerrilla strategy made it difficult for the Israel army to stop it. But what the military forces could not achieve, Ariel Sharon did. Once he became prime minister, a series of targeted assassinations started to disseminate the leaders of the resistance. Additionally, he imposed a strict control of the borders of Gaza, putting a greater strain on the Palestinians because the access to water was restricted, and a wall was built to blockade the use of fertile lands. In 2005, Sharon's plan to withdraw all Israeli life from Gaza, in order to impose a full blockade, extinguished the Intifada's flame.

What can we learn from this? This might sound like a broken disc but, once again, it must be repeated: no matter the differences between Israel's and Palestine's leaders, Palestinians are the ones who suffer. It is their lives that keep being ignored, and it is their future that is, as of right now, *blocked*.

The Iraq War (2003-2011)

A conflict between Iraq and the United States—endorsed by international forces—started in 2003 with the claim that the Iraqi government of Saddam Hussein was in control of weapons of mass destruction and that Hussein was linked to al-Qaeda. Even when Hussein's government was shattered after months of American invasion, an exhaustive search found no weapons, and yet the US only left until 2011. Losses were once again a stark projection of inequality: around 175 dead soldiers for the coalition, between 11,000 and 40,000 on the Iraqi side. That is without adding the close to 8,000 civilians' deaths.

Timeline:

- **September 11, 2001:** Four airplanes are used to attack the US, killing around 3,000 people. The blame rested on al-Qaeda and its leader Osama bin Laden, who was living in Afghanistan.
- **December 7, 2001:** The United States started a military operation in Afghanistan.
- **January 29, 2002:** George Bush presented The *axis of evil*, its members were identified as: Iraq, Iran and North Korea.
- **September 24, 2002:** The *Iraq Dossier* is published by the United Kingdom, stating that Saddam Hussein possesses weapons of mass destruction that can be activated in forty-five minutes.
- **November 8, 2002:** Resolution 1441 is passed by the United Nations Security Council granting Iraq an ultimatum to either comply with the disarmament or face serious consequences.
- **November-March 2003:** The UN carried out 700 research commissions in Iraq: no weapons of mass destruction were ever found.

- **February 25, 2003:** A draft resolution is presented by the US and the UK at the UN affirming that Iraq will not surrender peacefully. France, Russia and Germany oppose.
- **March, 20, 2003:** Operation Iraqi Freedom started.

Context: To understand the hurricane that wiped away a whole decade of development for the Iraqi population, it is necessary to go back to the first storm produced at the end of the Gulf War. Iraq had been forced to dismember its weapons of mass destruction and accept continuous inspections from the UN, a non-fly zone was also assessed. Oil exportation was prohibited under heavy economic sanctions, and it was only later allowed with the exclusive purpose of buying food and medicines in the framework of the UN's program Oil per Food—a program that was not free of corruption or abuse.

Even with the sanctions in place, the UK and the US bombarded the country in 1998. Once George Bush took over the presidency and the 9/11 attack happened, the cards for a bigger disaster were laid out.

The Invasion & the Occupation: On March 20, 2003, war erupted in Iraq. From the air and the sea bombs were causing mayhem on the ground, a mere appetizer for the arrival of troops of the coalition and the consequent annihilation of Iraqi forces. By April, the remnants of the Iraqi defense were falling to pieces and Saddam Hussein went missing, facilitating the capture of Baghdad by foreign invaders. It was May, and according to Bush marked the end of the conflict. However, the war was far from over.

The country had been swallowed by darkness, its society broken and the temporary government installed by the US and the UK did not improve the situation. In 2004 governing authority was reinstituted to Iraq. The international troops, however, stayed with the intention of hunting Hussein down and finding the so-called weapons of mass destruction. The fact that Saddam Hussein was captured in December 2003, convicted to death and executed by the end of 2006 did little to improve the conditions of the Iraqi society. Next, rebels occupied the national landscape and the fight between Shiites and Sunnites reached a violent stage, the perfect recipe for al-Qaeda to meddle.

What can we learn from it? Why was the US—albeit with the UK's support—so impatient to fight this war? We have covered the official reasons in the previous paragraphs, but does it really make sense? Why go against its usual allies (Europe) just for the sake of a hunch? The UK's *Dossier* was never corroborated, and no active weapons of mass destruction were ever found. This begs the question: was this the greatest intelligence failure in history, or was it just a falsehood?

Israel's Withdrawal from Gaza (2005)

What happened? Israel withdrew all its illegal settlements from the Gaza Strip on August 15, 2005, after occupying the area since the War of the Six-Days (1967). From that time, the Gaza Strip was invaded by twenty-one settlements and around 9,000 colonists. The reasons for this were linked to an increase in the costs of overseeing the zone and, indubitably, to a political display. To ensure no one doubted Israel's goodwill, the settlers who refused to leave were dragged out of their houses.

Today, six-teen years later, the Gaza Strip is still under Israel's control.

The story behind the script: The idea of pulling out the settlements was not a sudden one. In the days of the Second Intifada (2000-2005), Israel PM Ariel Sharon proposed a withdrawal from the Gaza Strip. With the arrival of the elections of 2003 and for campaign purposes, Sharon had a change of heart and declared his support for the continuous colonization of the Strip. Once he was reelected, his support shifted again. Sharon now was endorsing a departure from the Gaza Strip on the grounds of keeping Israelis safe and the armed forces relieved from such burden. The Israeli Parliament (Knesset) approved Sharon's plan, only Foreign Secretary Benjamin Netanyahu—who is currently serving as Prime Minister—voiced his thoughts against it, asking for a referendum. This changed when the leader of the PLO Yasser Arafat died in November 2004.

By February of the next year, the Knesset fully approved Sharon's strategy and in March it was announced that no Israeli citizen was allowed to settle in the Gaza Strip.

The Show: On August 15, 2005, Israeli forces walked in the Gush Katif area, following the order to officialize the settler's exit. In the face of being offered monetary compensation, some of them agreed, others refused and were literally dragged away from their homes. The images of children raising hands and holding the Star of David evoked bitter memories from the Holocaust around the world. The dramatic stage had been accomplished. Seven days later the evacuation was completed, and the Palestinians walked, for the first time in decades, around streets that used to be out of their reach.

Then reality hit.

Reality: Israeli faces were gone, yes, but their repression continued forcefully. Right in the middle of Palestine's September celebration, Israeli planes bombarded the Strip killing civilians and bringing down buildings that allegedly were used as a warehouse for the fabrication of weapons. A strict economic blockade followed.

In 2007, due to internal disputes between the political parties of Palestine Authority and Fatah, Israel completely sealed Gaza's frontiers, positioning its population under the abuse of a strict siege that is ongoing to this very day.

What we can learn from it. There is no denying that in politics, fictional scripts are usually the best diplomatic weapon. Obviously, Israel's government had this in mind when developing its strategy in leaving Gaza. What was the problem then? Diplomacy ends when death starts to accumulate. Leaving Gaza has not changed anything for the Palestinians, if anything, it has made things worse. The discriminatory control, lacking the presence of Israeli settlers in the area, is nowadays at its more ruthless.

The Lebanon-Israel War (2006)

Figures:

- It lasted thirty-three days, starting on July 12, 2006, and finishing in August 2014.
- Around 1,200 Lebanese died, mostly civilians, a third of them children.
- One third of Lebanon's population—4.5 million people—was left displaced.
- Forty-three Israeli civilians were killed.

How did it start? Everything began in July 2006, when Hezbollah—a Lebanese military and political group—decided to attack an Israeli patrol, killing two soldiers and kidnapping another two with the hopes of using them as bargaining chips. As it could be expected, Israel did not take this lightly, and soon both parties saw their territories swallowed by bombs and missiles that reduced cities to scattered ashes. Hezbollah launched more than 4,000 rockets directed to the north of Israel, while Israel dropped around 7,000 bombs and missiles in the south of Lebanon.

Background: When Israel withdrew its physical presence from Gaza, the situation of abuse and oppression did not improve. On the contrary, persecution against Palestinians was part of the routine. It was precisely at this moment that an exchange of violence happened, with Israeli forces abducting civilians and Palestinian militia taking two Israel soldiers in retaliation. Israel's next move? To arrest over thirty

Palestinian politicians who allegedly had links with Hamas. Following this, Hezbollah decided to intervene in favor of Palestine.

Who won? This question remains difficult to answer since both sides claimed victory. For Hezbollah, the war represented the fact that it was possible to face the most powerful army in the Middle East. For Israel, however, victory was not military. Their goal of rescuing their soldiers alive was unfulfilled and Hezbollah came out stronger than it was before. The only thing that Israel did was not be defeated.

Reflections: The narrative of success might be different from one side to the other. Nevertheless, there is something that remains clear: it was the Lebanese society that suffered the most in the aftermath of the war. The infrastructure of the country was literally burned down. The repairing costs have been calculated to be at $3.5 billion, since bridges, buildings, roads, among other structures were completely destroyed. Even nowadays, locals face the latent threat posed by the unexploded bombs that remain in the southern part of Lebanon.

The Arab Spring in the Middle East (2010)

This chapter is going to be a little different, because it will be devoted to remembering how the movement that brought the Middle East and North Africa to the brink of a social revolution started, and analyzing how palpable change was implemented in the countries involved.

The Origin: The calendar marked December 10, when a street vendor in Tunisia, called Mohamed Bouazizi, set his body on fire as a demonstration to call attention to the dramatically poor living conditions in his country. Thousands of protesters followed his example by filling up the Tunisian streets. Through this, they expressed being a society who could not and would not stand more abuse. Subsequently, the dictator Ben Ali was dethroned and soon the victory of Tunisia was a call for action across the Middle East. If democracy had been given to the people, they would seek it through their voices. Or this was the plan.

Yemen: The situation seemed hopeful, the dictator Ali Abdulá Saleh was removed from power and following a popular referendum Mansour Hadi was legally recognized president of Yemen. At least he was until Saleh rejected the results and found in the Houthi a temporary ally to force Hadi to resign and to seek the protection of Saudi Arabia. From this, Saudi Arabia has fabricated a humanitarian disaster for the Yemeni population, with the justification of having the duty to annihilate the Houthi power. The initial hope was hollow.

Bahrain: The narrative advanced along these lines: A Shiite majority demanded reforms and social parity from the Sunnite ruling monarchy. The response from the monarchy? Violence and blood. For the Bahrain government, the social demand was a plot orchestrated by Iran, the level of repression was justified. Ten years down the line, in 2020, a different Crown Prince, Sheikh Salman bin Hamad al-Khalifa, was appointed prime minister. While al-Khalifa is praised for his reform-minded personality and a moderate style of governing, there is a factor that cannot be changed: Bahrain's dependence on Saudi Arabia, a country that has long supported the Sunnite monarchy.

Syria: This case is so horrific, a war turned into a humanitarian mayhem that is still going after ten years. As such, it deserves to have its own chapter, which can be found right after this one.

The Syrian Civil War (2001-Present)

What's happening: When the Arab Spring broke out in the Middle East, words such as "hope" and "change" were used continuously. People from Tunisia to Egypt stood up for the recovery of their rights in the face of non-democratic leaders. Amidst the movement, Syria was supposed to be one of the many cases of relative success. Just a couple of months before the publishing of this book, the 10th anniversary of the Syria War was remembered and not celebrated because it deems impossible to do so while blood keeps pouring from Syrians and chaos keeps ruling at the hands of Bashar al-Assad. The last attempt to register an official tally of how many people have been killed was in 2016 and, by then, half a million people had died because of the war. More than half the pre-war population of 23 million remains displaced, 90% of Syrians survive under extreme poverty, the rate is the same for the amount of children who need humanitarian assistance. However, no one seems interested enough to do anything about it.

How did it start? The al-Assad family has ruled Syria for the last forty years. They belong to a minority called Shiite in a country where most of its population are Sunnites and there is an important presence of Kurds in the north, right where rich plants of oil are abundant. The population seemed resigned with the status quo since no protests had ever challenged Bashar al-Assad's power, who had been in office since 2000. In 2011 this was about to change.

In March of that year, adolescents were arrested and tortured in the city of Daraa for painting pro-democracy graffiti. Manifestations flared up in the country and by March 15 they expanded to Damascus, the capital of Syria. The reaction of the government was to crush down the opposition by detaining and killing. In October, deserters from the Syrian Army created the Free Syrian Army as a way to respond against the brutality of al-Assad. The armed fight had started.

On the very first day the government launched the attack, 200 people were murdered and the city of Homs was devastated by weapons designed for large-scale conflicts. Aleppo was sieged and Idlib was captured. By the end of 2011 more than 4,000 people had died and the first wave of refugees desperately sought shelter in Turkey, Jordan and Lebanon.

External Players & ISIS: While it is common knowledge to talk about the Syrian War as a civil conflict (from the beginning it was clear that the international community was seeing the country as a chessboard where interests could be quickly traded), Syrian rebels were supported by Turkey in an attempt to stop the advance of al-Assad and, at the same time, gain momentum against the protagonist of the Kurds. Assad let al-Qaeda members out of jail in a nod to the so-called religious forces that were backing him up. The Gulf countries were quick in financing those forces just for the sake of keeping their conservative interests strong. The UN's attempts to promote cease-fires failed due to the veto power of Russia and China. Russia presented unconditional support to Bashar al-Assad, not only politically but militarily. Russian aircraft bombarded Syrian cities held by rebels. ISIS came out of Iraq and by 2013 it was freely operating in Syria, the Caliphate installed in the city of Raqqa, making it the main attraction for jihadists across the world.

Chemical Weapons & Barack Obama's failure: The United States had made a promise under Barack Obama's leadership: if the government of Bashar al-Assad used chemical weapons against civilians, then the 'leader of the free world' would authorize a military intervention against the Syrian regime. In 2011, that regime gassed civilians, the first in a long row of chemical attacks that killed 1,500 people, if not more. Obama ignored this, failing to act. Naturally, al-Assad did not care either.

It would be Donald Trump in 2017 and 2018 who finally sent aircraft, albeit limited to the areas where the Kurds were fighting against the advance of ISIS. By 2019, the US was already withdrawing from Syria.

What can we learn from it? There is a saying somewhere that assures that the last thing a human might lose is hope. Once this is lost, life cannot be retrieved. Ten years of hell have brought Syria to a point of no return. In the midst of the worst, Syrians would ask journalists: Why does no one care about us? Is help to come?

Now, there is only silence.

The Killing of Osama bin Laden (2011)

Timeline:

2007: US Intelligence obtains Osama's name from one of his most trusted men

2009: The area where that bin Laden and his family lives is located in Pakistan

August 2010: US Intelligence identifies the Abbottabad Complex as bin Laden's residence. It is brought to notice that this house is valued at 1 million USD. Hence, it is suspected that Osama bin Laden might be living there.

March 2011: President Obama oversees the first of five meetings of the National Security Council to discuss the attack on Abbottabad.

April 29, 2011: Obama gives green light to the operation.

May 2, 2011: The attack on Abbottabad is carried out by twenty-five Navy SEALs. Three men, including Osama's son, die and the body of bin Laden is identified.

The Story: There is nothing more effective to bond people together than national pride. For Americans the day when the al-Qaeda leader, responsible for the attacks of September 11, 2001, was pronounced dead was a day of celebration and demonstration of victory for the US. However, as years have passed, information from high ranked officials in the Intelligence department has hinted that instead of a deep strategy, the operation was more a matter of sheer luck and gambling. The risk was on how uncertain the data that led to the attack was. For former CIA Director John Brennan, the operation had many factors against its success. Firstly, the amount of evidence and sources of information were not reliable. Secondly, it was dubious how legal the operation was, because hunting a man whose nationality is not

American and who lives in a third party nation, remains an issue of debate among human rights scholars today.

Questions: In 2015, Pulitzer Winner Seymour Hersh published an article in the *London Review of Books*. According to his research, many of the facts surrounding bin Laden's death were fictionalized. For starters, he argued that it was not the CIA that discovered the information about bin Laden's location, instead, the intel came from an agent who belonged to the Intelligence Forces of Pakistan. Hersh's testimony proposed a completely different version and explanation for what happened in the Abbottabad Complex: Pakistan had allegedly captured Osama bin Laden way back in 2006 and had kept him as captive in Abbottabad, a military complex 3km away from the General Academy of the National Army. The health of the terrorist leader had been weakened, and he lived as a prisoner of the Pakistani state. Once the US found out about his whereabouts they merely trampled over Pakistan and executed Osama bin Laden on the spot.

Consequences: Regardless of how it happened, the murder of Osama bin Laden was a magnificent moment of victory for the United States. For Barack Obama it meant a political achievement that led him to reelection to the presidency in 2012. As for al-Qaeda, the blow was more personal than strategic considering that they had already lost control over Afghanistan and their networks were dismantled before bin Laden's death. Osama bin Laden was soon replaced by Ayman al-Zawahiri, who although not as charismatic and inspiring to his followers, has moved al-Qaeda in a direction that would have never been taken under bin Laden's watch: the decentralization of jihadist operations.

What can we learn from it? Ten years after Osama bin Laden's death, many questions remain unanswered. When leaving legal matters aside, there is one question that intelligence services around the world should consider: How effective is it to kill a terrorist leader? Does it actually change something in the world or even within the region? Or is it just political propaganda designed for the benefit of a few?

Yemeni Civil War (2014-Present)

What is happening? The United Nations has described the situation as one of the worst humanitarian disasters of recent history. The War has resulted in 24 million people in need of assistance, at least 250,000 deaths either directly or indirectly (lack of food, poor health services and damaged infrastructure), famine is around the corner and the situation worsens by the minute. This is the summary of a war that started as an internal conflict in 2014 between the Houthi movement and government forces, and was submitted to international intervention—mainly Saudi Arabia's—with the purpose of fighting against Iranian-backed Houthi rebels. The coalition led by Saudi Arabia (United Arab Emirates, Kuwait, Qatar and Egypt) got involved with the intention of ceasing the clash, but all these years have proven that such a purpose was never fulfilled or respected. Additionally, the presence of the coalition has only deepened the polarization within the country.

Context: While the roots of the conflict are commonly adjudicated to the Houthis, the origins truly rely on the aftermath of the Arab Spring when in 2011 the authoritarian president Ali Abdullah Saleh was forced to hand out his power to a deputy, Abdrabbuh Mansour Hadir. Once Mr Hadi was the president, the country fared no better. Hadi's attempt to govern was haunted by jihadists attacking, voices of separation in the south, corruption and food scarcity.

The Houthi, representatives of Yement's Zaidi Shia Muslim minority, had already battled against Saleh and had noted Mr Hadi's incapacity as an opportunity to have full control over the north of the capital, Sanaa. But they were not alone, many Yemenis felt disappointed and frustrated over the disgracing situation of their country and found in the Houthis a way to voice out their lack of hope for a better tomorrow. By 2015, the Houthi movement controlled Sanaa.

Strengthened by the opportunist support of former president Saleh, the Houthis almost managed to carry through their desire of taking over the whole country by forcing Mr Hadi to leave Yemen in March 2015.

Saudi Arabia & the start of an unending war: This action would ignite panic in Saudi Arabia. Saudis believed that the Houthis were backed by the Shias in Iran—something that has yet to be confirmed. Saudi Arabia, a Sunni nation, gathered eight Arab states in a coalition in order to both put an end to the advances of the Houthis and restore Mr Hadi to a puppet government, since it had no power whatsoever in the country. After a temporary relocation in the Yemeni city of Aden, Mr Hadi had to go to Saudi Arabia.

The alliance between the Houthis and Mr Saleh was broken in 2017, when Saleh asked his followers to rise against the Houthis, in consequence, he was killed. Although the coalition—with the support of the US, UK and France—planned for the intervention to only last a couple of weeks, its actions differed from a real search for dialogue and peace. The Houthis lost ground in the south, but they still have a stronghold in the north. Both ends of the country are continuously assaulted regardless of the presence of civilians. In the same manner, terrorist forces like al-Qaeda have made their way into areas of the neglected south. To make things worse, Gulf countries led by Saudi Arabia have maintained a strong economic blockade over Yemen.

A humanitarian disaster & the US's role: It is no secret that the US has supported Saudi Arabia's invasion of Yemen. The reasons for this range from strategic geopolitics in the Gulf to the obvious enormous oil power the Kingdom of Saudi Arabia holds. The association is based upon mutual benefit: the US is able to expand its counterterrorism agenda on Yemeni ground, and, in return, Saudi Arabia manages to cast a veil over the atrocities of its participation in a war that was never theirs to fight. Back in 2018 when a school bus was bombarded in Yemen killing forty-four kids by a Saudi jet, the bombs carried the

American flag. Current President Joe Biden announced that the US would no longer provide military support to Saudi Arabia, yet he also stated that they could be used for *defense* purposes. Where is the line between defense and attack? It has not been made clear. In the meantime, a country is destroyed and millions of people are at risk of famine, including children who only eat one meal per day, if they are lucky—their fate relies heavily on humanitarian aid and a broken health system.

What can we learn from it? There are more than thirty fronts ravaging Yemen. The country is seen as a chessboard where global players move pieces with only one goal in mind: convenience. Iran and Saudi Arabia see Yemen as their playground, forgetting it is a matter of survival versus deaths for the Yemenis. As for the international community, with the US at its head, aside from delivering delayed packages of humanitarian aid, there is no interest to rush the movement of the next pawn.

Killing of Jamal Khashoggi (2018)

What happened? On October 2, 2018, Jamal Khashoggi, a Saudi journalist based in the US walked in the Saudi consulate in Istanbul in need to sort out paperwork, since he was planning to marry his Turkish girlfriend.

He never left the building. Jamal Khashoggi was murdered by Saudi forces by order of Saudi Crown Prince Mohammed bin Salman. The records obtained by Turkish intelligence were proof for how brutal Mr Khashoggi's death was. He was dismembered.

Who was Jamal Khashoggi? The fifty-nine-year-old journalist had worked for the Saudi media covering important stories such as the Soviet invasion in Afghanistan and the rise to power of al-Qaeda leader Osama bin Laden. He also had a close relationship with the Saudi government and worked as an adviser. Something changed in their relationship and Khashoggi moved to the US, from where he wrote as a columnist of the *Washington Post*, criticizing the policies of the Crown Prince. In his own writings, Mr Khashoggi communicated that he feared for his life.

What Saudi Arabia said? For weeks and in spite of the clear link, the Kingdom denied any involvement in the journalist's murder. Later statements implied that Mr Khashoggi had died during a fight after refusing deportation to Saudi Arabia or from an accidental chokehold. The final declaration linked the event to *rogue* Saudi agents, rejecting any association with the Crown Prince. Five of the supposedly men implied assured they acted on their own accord. International observers of human rights demanded a further investigation regarding the involvement of Mohammed bin Salman, as it was clear that the assassination had happened under Saudi Arabia's responsibility.

What the US found and what Biden did not do. A US Intelligence report released this February found Crown Prince bin Salman responsible for approving Jamal Khashoggi's execution. Travel restrictions were set for subjects believed to have a connection to the Khashoggi's case but not on the prince himself. This left Biden in an uncomfortable position, because during his campaign he had promised that if the US ever found the Crown Prince responsible for the murder, he would be held accountable.

What we can learn from it. Nothing of what has been done or can be done will change the fact that a man, a journalist, was murdered in the grounds of a consulate. Mr Khashoggi will not be coming back to life, but if Saudi Arabia is not held responsible, the reasons as for why he was killed might return to end the life of someone else who dares speak out against a prince.

Lebanon's Socio-Economic Crisis (2019-Present)

What's happening? On August 4, 2020, a brutal explosion in Beirut, Lebanon provoked the death of over 130 people, injured 5,000, and left 300,000 homeless. The disaster happened in a chemical warehouse that stored 2,750 tons of ammonium nitrate in unsafe conditions. A horrible accident that should have been prevented. The perfect analogy for the situation of the country as a whole. Lebanon's economic collapse can be summarized in the following way: corruption and a succession of disasters that cover the political arena, a refugee crisis, a crumbling economy and of course, COVID-19.

Why did it happen? After a civil war that left Beirut in a collection of debris and poverty, skyscrapers and shopping malls with international spirits started to fill the landscape. Where did the money come from? Creditors. Tons of creditors. Lebanon's financial system has achieved something completely unexpected: it has turned the development of a country into a Ponzi scheme. Hence, the government obtains money by asking for credits and loans that, in turn, is used to pay other creditors. Their guarantee? Nothing but their human capital—that is, millions of Lebanese who would go abroad to find work and send money back to home. Even in the midst of the financial crisis of 2008, the plan seemed to work, and to that it was added the support of the Gulf countries that bolstered the reserves of the Lebanese Central Bank. Therefore, Lebanon thought itself secure, until the arrival of 2011.

Gulf Countries walking away and the banks' last scheme: As a consequence of both the Arab Spring and the fact that Hezbollah was gaining momentum with the support of Iran, the Gulf countries stopped seeing Lebanon as an ally. Thus, the boost that kept the Central Bank functioning was no more. But in 2016, banks started offering impressive interest rates for new deposits of dollars—which happens to be an official currency—and Lebanese pounds. The logic behind this was that considering that the Lebanese pound had kept a stable value compared to the dollar for twenty years, nothing could go wrong and dollars would keep going in.

Taxing WhatsApp calls and the collapse: Remember the movies set in the Middle Ages and how they tend to portray an evil king who, for the sake of keeping appearances and attending balls every night, raises taxes on everything? Well, that is more or less the case for what the Lebanese state did in 2018 and later in 2019. In October 2019, the government came up with a plan: taxing WhatsApp calls. Now, let's remember another fact: the millions of Lebanese who live and work abroad. How would their relatives (who were already heavily affected by poverty) keep in touch with them if something free suddenly became a luxury?

Mass protests and a disastrous drop of the currency: The ludicrous proposal of the government set fire amongst the Lebanese youth. The protests were not just about keeping WhatsApp free, it was about demanding a governmental structural change. They refused to be part of more damaging schemes. In consequence, dollars flew away from Lebanon. To save what was left, banks closed their doors and cashiers became unavailable. People who had kept their savings and salaries there were left with nothing. The stable relationship the Lebanese pound had with the dollar crumbled apart as the national currency collapsed, going up to the staggering value of 8,000 per dollar.

The worst time for the worst health crisis: Even before the Beirut accident, half of the Lebanese population lived in poverty, the middle class was nonexistent, and acquiring food became a daunting task due to the fact that 80% of products come from other countries. The explosion in Beirut and the billions of dollars left in damage were already enough of a threat to a public health system that for years had been surviving on the brink of collapse. The straw that broke the camel's back came with the arrival of Covid-19, creating a new chapter of horror in Lebanon. After the explosion, fifteen health centers in

Beirut were so affected that it remains, even now, impossible to provide the attention people need. Social restrictions, while necessary, pushed the population to a new level of despair, as hundreds of businesses were forced to close.

Chapter VI: North America

Antranik Artinian

David Xu

The Cold War (1947-1991)

By David Xu

American foreign policy towards the Soviet Union under Reagan:

Ronald Reagan was the 40th President of the United States and, in many ways, he made a tremendous impact on the history leading up to the collapse of the Soviet Union. Yet, the continuity of Reagan's Foreign Policy has been widely contested, as he was far less aggressive towards the Soviet Union from 1985 upwards. To examine the consistency of Reagan's foreign policy, this essay will cover: 1) Reagan's foreign policy approaches; 2) the shift in Reagan's foreign policy; 3) the level of consistency in Reagan's foreign policy; and 4) the degree of the changes of Reagan's foreign policy. I will argue that the changes in the Reagan administration's foreign policy were very much overstated, since the administration was consistent with his foreign policy aim of restoring American dominance and rolling back Soviet aggression at a reasonable cost.

To fully understand Reagan's foreign policy narrative, one must first look at the context in which Reagan was elected president. The 1970s was a challenging decade for America on many fronts. Economically, America had a high inflation rate with worsening economic performances (Frum 2000, 290-295). GDP growth in the United States failed drastically, from around 5.5% in 1973 to a jaw-dropping -0.25% in 1979 (World Bank, n.d.). Adding the 1979 Iranian Revolution into the mix, the United States was faced with yet another energy crisis within the same decade (Tran 2009). Politically, the public had not yet fully recovered from the trauma of Vietnam. Internationally, the hawkish Soviet Union, under Brezhnev, had also raised some serious doubts amongst the public, namely, the right-wing conservatives about the validity of the Détente. As a result, President Carter's leadership was put into serious question. The troubled 1979 was well summarized by President Carter' famous Malaise speech where he stated that Washington faced a serious 'crisis of confidence'

(Carter 1979). Bear in mind that this was before the Iranian hostage crisis in November (BBC 1979) and the Soviet Invasion of Afghanistan in December (BBC 2019). Then comes Ronald Reagan.

Reagan's 1980 presidential election forever keyed the phrase 'Let's Make America Great Again' into history. The landslide victory of Ronald Reagan truly embodied the rising of right-wing politics in the United States. Economically, Reagan promised a balanced budget. He blamed government expenditure as the main cause behind the high inflation rate. This was the result of an overreaching federal government (Reagan 1980). Hence, Reagan promised tax cuts as he was a firm believer of trickle-down economics. Foreign policy-wise, Reagan promised to rebuild the American military capability to push back the ever so expanding Soviet aggression (Cannon 1980). Reagan enjoyed a landslide victory and with the American hostages released the day of his inauguration, he was able to fully commit to war against the 'evil empire' (Reagan 1983). What Reagan left unanswered was how he would achieve an extraordinary military build-up while maintaining low government expenditure.

The short answer is that Reagan never did. To defeat the 'Evil Empire' (Reagan 1983), Reagan adopted a hawkish position towards the Soviet Union and its Third World allies. Reagan's administration saw a huge increase in defense spending, much of it was dedicated to research and development (Reagan 1985). The high military expenditure fulfilled Reagan's campaign promises and allowed him to present a hawkish posture.

Government expenditure rose drastically under the Reagan administration, roughly 14% in 1981 alone. Annually, more than 25% of the Reagan administration government expenditure was directed at military spending (Executive Office of the President of the United States 2013, 193). By having such high military expenditure, not only did the Reagan administration inject considerable capital into the domestic economy, but it was also a major step to restore the dominance of the American military. One of the rationales behind such build-up is that increasing defense spending was the only way for the

US to match the high Soviet military expenditure, a common view shared by many neo-conservatives at the time (Pipe 1981, 208-212). Chernoff also argued that the arms race made it unaffordable for Soviets to continue its long-established militaristic foreign policy, a way to force the Soviets to negotiate (Chernoff 1991, 114; NSDD-66, 1983).

Reagan's administration emphasized strategic balance aimed at the Soviet military modernization to enlarge its negotiating leverages. These guiding principles led to an unprecedented level of military preparation for both America and its allies in Europe. Domestically, the Reagan administration enlarged the numbers of military personnel, the numbers of battleships and fighter jets. Internationally, the most famous example is the deployment of nuclear Pershing II IRBMs and cruise missiles, the Euromissiles project. This is an American led counter-offensive to equip its NATO allies against the Soviet deployment of SS-20s (Busch 1997, 450-455). The Soviet aggression perceived by the Reagan administration was valid. SS-20s was an advanced Soviet mobile missile launcher of the time. Each vehicle had the capacity of launching three warheads. With 252 launchers in place, it allowed the Soviet military to simultaneously strike 756 targets, even before reloading (The New York Times 1983).

Yet, what should also be noted is that the Soviet's military expenditure at the time was greatly overestimated. The military spending of the Soviet Union was in no way transparent at the time. Hence, the Central Intelligence Agency (CIA) was the only one capable of assessing Soviet military expenditure. However, several revisions were made, with one being a full scale recalculation due to the wrong conversion between the currencies. This created a false notion of high Soviet military expenditure and was not corrected until 1983. The CIA admitted that the annual growth of Soviet defense spending was around 2% rather than 5% in the previous assessment, far lower to that of the 6% average annual increase of the American military spending growth up to 1986. In real terms, Soviet military spending was more than 100 billion dollars less than the US in the 1980s. (Chernoff 1991, 114-122)

Besides the conventional military build-up, the Reagan administration also wished to improve the technological military capacity. One of the most highlighted projects being the strategic defense initiative (SDI), aka Reagan's Star War project. Essentially, the hope was to construct a satellite nuclear defense system in space against the potential Soviet warheads. Reagan had long been interested in the uses of laser technology. While he was the governor in 1967, he was frequently briefed on the research and development of *Direct Energy Weapons* by Dr. Teller of the Lawrence Livermore laboratory (The Atomic Heritage Foundation 2018). Upon arriving at the Oval Office, Reagan formalized his interests in SDI through directing giant sums of research funding in his National Security Decision Directive (NSDD) in 1981 (The White House 1981). Reagan formally announced SDI in 1983 (Reagan, 1983). The development of SDI linked closely with Reagan's unconventional thinking of breaking free from nuclear deterrence, a project with the capacity of seriously undermining the principle of mutually assured destruction (MAD) upon the first strike (Fischer 2010, 277-280). It should also be noted that although this was not the driving force behind Reagan's foreign policy, it also fits the narrative of the 1983 nuclear freezing campaign (Winter 2010).

Reagan's costly Stars War program quickly drew the attention of Moscow. The reason being that the SDI could trump the long-established concept of MAD. Without the guaranteed consequences of retaliation, it would be far more likely for one to launch the deadly first strike. In theory, this is a valid concern, but in reality, no one at the time could guarantee the practicality of the SDI. Even if the United States was able to create such a defense mechanism, there were several available strategies for the Soviet Union to bypass such a system (Westwick 2008, 955-957). Back then, Moscow was increasingly concerned with the development and the possible launch of SDI. The Soviet obsession with SDI stemmed from the fact that 'if

Americans oversold it [SDI], we Russians overbought it' (Sagadeev 1994). Despite the somewhat fictional nature of SDI, diplomatically, the Russian's obsessions with SDI offered the Reagan administration huge leverage when it came to the later negotiations. But this is also to say that Reagan himself was a true believer of SDI and his administration continued the SDI project until his very last day in office (Westwick 2008, 955-957).

Reagan's Third World offensive is very costly, but affordable, as it minimized the use of American forces, making him a 'peace-loving' hawk (Beinart 2010). Reagan's foreign policy towards the Third World is designed to roll back the Soviet aggression through supporting anti-communist political entities by any means necessary, a core element of the Reagan doctrine. It should also be pointed out that Reagan neglected the key American value of human rights, showing his pragmatic nature (Pach 2006).

Reagan's Third World policy relied heavily on the use of financial capitals and the American intelligence community. The model was first established after the Soviet invasion of Afghanistan. Upon arriving at the Oval Office, President Reagan was faced with the choice of either putting boots on the ground or sending arms to the Afghan opposition, the Mujahideen. Reagan's administration went with the latter option. Code-named Operation Cyclone, American aid to Mujahideen was largely carried out by the then CIA director William Casey who was one of the first Director of Central Intelligence (DCI) to receive a cabinet status, which allowed him a far greater ability to coordinate Reagan's war against the Soviet in the Third World. Casey flew frequently to Pakistan to visit the then President Muhammed Zia-ul Haq and provided the Pakistani government with billions of dollars' worth of both economic and military aid for its war against the Democratic Republic of Afghanistan, which were backed by the Soviet. This includes some of the more advanced military equipment including stinger missiles and F16 fighter jets. The initial objective until 1984 was simply for the insurgency to disrupt and to make the war for the Soviets costlier (Riedel 2014, 110-127).

Latin America was also the forefront of President Reagan's long pledged support for anti-communist insurgency worldwide. To do so, the Reagan administration sponsored the Nicaraguan anti-communist insurgency (the Contras) both economically and militarily. Then came the Boland Amendment I and II which made it illegal for American funding of the right-wing rebels, the Contras, who were fighting to overthrow the ruling government in Nicaragua (NSC 1985). The Reagan administration lobbied the congress and acquired direct humanitarian aid for the Contras. The support of the Contras concluded with the press discovery of the Iran-Contra Affairs in 1986 (Brown University n.d.)

The preference for the financing of the rebel group in the Third World reflected the anti-war sentiment at the time (Kindig 2008). The general public made up many of his supporters, all of which heavily opposed direct American interference, even if it meant that the United States would lose to the Soviets. (Beinart 2010). The only two large-scale military operations carried out during the Reagan administration were the invasion of Grenada and the peacekeeping mission by the multinational force in Lebanon. Operation Urgent Fury was very much a bully mission by the American military against the Grenadian forces. American forces, along with local militias and Jamaican forces, were able to take over in less than a week (Clarke n.d.). The peacekeeping mission in Lebanon was short-lived as well. President Reagan quickly withdrew the American forces after the suicide bombing attack against the MNF barrack that killed more than 240 marines in 1983 (Wright 2019).

The shift of Reagan's foreign policy refers to his softer approaches with the Soviet Union from 1983, including the later negotiation. The shift was consistent with his previous political narrative. Rather than calling it a remake, it was more like the sequel of the first term of Reagan's foreign policy. This transition very much revealed President Reagan's true colors as an opportunistic pragmatist. (Pach 2006).

Reagan's pivot can be seen in 1983, but no substantial cooperation took place until 1985. In 1985, Reagan had already won the election for his second term and America was ahead of the Soviets both economically and militarily. This allowed him to negotiate from a point of strength and, most importantly, he got the long-awaited end of the Brezhnev era. The death of Brezhnev in 1982 was very much a downturn of Soviet aggression (The New York Times 1982). Despite the cozying up from both sides of the conflict, due to the death of three leaders within a little more than two and a half years, nothing concrete was settled until 1985. Mikhail Gorbachev took office in 1985 and announced rapid reforms. Perestroika, aka, the economic restructuring, was the main political agenda of the Gorbachev era. It was an attempt to liberalize the market into a managed economy. The move allowed joint ventures with foreign capitals to attract Foreign Direct Investment (FDI), rejuvenating the Soviet economy. It was an attempt to balance the high inflation rate of the previous decades. Gorbachev had hoped to redirect the finances from the costly arms race to the domestic economy, adding more capital to lift the Soviet Union out of the hyperinflation of the time (Brown 1997). With Gorbachev's rise to power, the Geneva Summit took place in 1985 and, subsequently, in 1986, the Reykjavík Summit occurred. The Reykjavík Summit was an overall success as both sides established constructive partnerships, Reagan and Gorbachev came close to reducing and even abandoning nuclear weapons and bypassing the concept of MAD once for all. However, the pair failed to reach an agreement due to Reagan's insistence on the testing of SDI (Matlock 2004). With the signing of the "Intermediate-Range Nuclear Force Treaty" (INF), Reagan's milder approaches towards the Soviets eventually yielded results in 1987 (SIPRI Yearbook 2007, 683). This was a crucial step in achieving Reagan's hope of stability beyond nuclear deterrence (Fischer 2010, 277-280), an agenda first published in NSDD-32 back in 1983 (NSDD-32, 1983).

Reagan's Reykjavík Summit with Gorbachev was a betrayal to the anti-communist faction within the United States, but this transition did not compromise Reagan's initial pledge to roll back the Soviet aggression (Reagan 1985). It was never Reagan's goal to defeat, let alone, destroy the Soviet Union (Fischer, 2010, 276). Reagan was very responsive to public sentiment throughout his presidency. During the 1980 presidential election, Reagan heavily criticized the Carter administration's dovish foreign policy. Reagan portrayed himself as a hawkish figure that fit the anti-communist sentiment of the time, and that was exactly what won him the Oval Office (Nincic 1990, 376). Yet, Reagan had been a peace-loving hawk, a character reflected in his constant refusal to use force to facilitate the anti-communist rhetoric in the Third World. Early on in Reagan's presidency, Secretary Alexander Haig advised Reagan to bomb Cuba to stop them from sponsoring the Nicaraguan communist regime. The idea terrified Reagan, who later pushed Haig out for his unrestricted confrontational policy (Beinart, 2010). It is crucial to note that despite the great level of public resentment towards the Soviet Union, Americans did not want to be dragged into another war, much less, a direct armed conflict with the Soviets (Nincic 1990, 376). Privately, Reagan had also disclosed his desire of building constructive cooperation with the Soviet Union as early as 1983, and even establishing an advisory group for that very purpose (Fischer 2010, 272).

    Reagan's State of the Union address in 1985 saw the emergence of the term Reagan Doctrine early on in Reagan's second term. Despite the late arrival of the term, it was a continuity of Reagan's first term, foreign policy, stating his firm support for the anti-communist insurgencies globally. This very address saw Reagan declaring his long-held desire since 1981 of 'seeking fair and verifiable arms agreements (with the Soviet Union) that would lower the risk of war and reduce the size of nuclear arsenals' (Reagan 1985) seven months before the Geneva Summit. Although the attitude towards the Soviet Union shifted slightly in the eyes of the public, Reagan continued many of his initial practices during his second term in office. Firstly, the military expenditure was still significantly higher compared to that of the Soviet's (Chernoff 1991, 114-122). Secondly, Reagan still held firm ground on the continuous research on the SDI, hoping that the Star War project would one day turn into a reality. Thirdly, his administration still vigorously supported the anti-communist rebel groups around the world, namely the Contras (Brown University, n.d.).

Many have also suggested that 1983 was a major transition in Reagan's thinking and that the preceding rapid events had made a huge impact on Reagan's foreign policy philosophy. The timing of Reagan's shift accurately reflected the concerns of America's European allies, namely the North Atlantic Treaty Organization (NATO). 1983 saw the American deployment of Euromissiles, the development of which were directly appealed by NATO, due to the fact that they would be first in line to face the Soviet's retaliation. (Fischer 2010, 274) In 1983, American forces, along with the American military, conducted routine Defense Readiness Condition (DEFCON) level 1 exercises, simulating an incoming nuclear attack from the Soviet Union, the Able Archer 83. Due to the rapid deterioration of the relations amongst the global forces, although initially discounted, it was later revealed to President Reagan by DCI William J. Casey in 1984 that the Soviet politburo speculated the nature of Able Archer 83 was a cover for an actual American first strike (Fischer n.d.). This had alarmed Reagan during previous confrontational approaches with the Soviet Union.

Reagan's transition came as a surprise to everyone, as he was a hard-line anti-communist when he was first elected to office back in 1981. Thus, the events leading up to the initial transition of approaches in Reagan's foreign policy towards the Soviets in 1983 were the result of a fundamental reorientation of Reagan's originally extreme approaches (Steinbrunner as cited in Gelb 1984). Reagan believed that the rapid military build-up and hard-line approaches had resulted in an unprecedented level of hostility. There were no rewards that could justify the level of risk Reagan's diehard approaches were bringing about. The near-miss of Able Archer 83 was merely one of the sobering moments for the Reagan administration that served as a reminder that the doomsday scenario of a full-on Russo-American war could be just around the corner (Fischer 2010, 273). Hence, the foreign policy transition from 1983 onwards was a key moment in the history of the Cold War and of Reagan's presidency.

In my view, this argument is deeply flawed. Although it was not disclosed publicly until 1985, Reagan had long held a desire to form constructive cooperation with the Soviet Union, a partnership that would have allowed him to achieve stability beyond nukes. As it was previously pointed out, Reagan's discreteness of his yearning for cooperation was a way for him to protect his public image (Nincic 1990, 376). This meant that Reagan could not publicly seek cooperation with the Soviet Union before his second term election, which also explains the timing of the Geneva summit. It could be argued that it is crucial to acknowledge the role of the mounting hostility in the pivot of Reagan's foreign policy but, like the constantly changing international environment at the time, it merely served as a warning for Reagan to recalibrate the degree of his hard-lined approaches towards the Soviet Union. The narrative had long been that Washington needed to find a stable coexistence with the Soviet Union in order to create a bipolar international order.

Bear in mind that it is extremely dangerous to look at history in retrospect. The collapse of the Soviet Union resulted in the rapid reforms of Gorbachev, which came across as a surprise to everyone. One could then contend that the attitudinal transition of Reagan's foreign policy would have been instrumental in facilitating a stable coexistence with the Soviet Union for decades to come. This is a valid argument, but it does not prove a fundamental doctrine reorientation of Reagan's foreign policy.

To conclude, Reagan was consistent with his foreign policy agenda of restoring American dominance and rolling back the increasing Soviet aggression at a reasonable cost throughout his presidency. The Reagan administration continued many of the initial confrontational policies, including the firm support of anti-communist insurgencies in the Third World till the end of Reagan's presidency. Reagan's pivot from 1983 onwards would appear to be a serious transition in public perception, however, it is most certainly an overstatement to assert that Reagan fundamentally changed his foreign policy's ideology. Negotiating with the Soviet Union was something Reagan had already been thinking about early on. All along, Reagan had been waiting for an ideal moment to negotiate with a reasonable Soviet leader from an advantageous position. By negotiating with the Soviets, the Reagan administration would firmly establish constructive cooperation between the two superpowers and rebuild a stable dichotomic international order for decades to come.

Early 1980's Recession

By Antranik Artinian

Oil Embargo & the 1973-1975 Recession: The OPEC's (Organization of the Petroleum Exporting Countries) oil embargo was a unanimous decision to stop exporting oil and fossil fuel to the US. This malaise was the result of President Nixon's decision to stop operating with the gold standard, as well as the US's military support to Israel — a strong tie that Arab countries are not fond of. Most OPEC members were affected by the ban removal of the gold standard since most of their assets were valued in US Dollars. As a result, Arab countries took Nixon's decision as a political warning. Subsequently, oil prices quadrupled from $2.90/barrel to $11.65/barrel between 1970 and 1974. This increase in prices was coupled by the high government spending on the Vietnam War, leading to high unemployment and inflation rates (a phenomenon called "stagflation").

What happened? In 1980, the US was prompted to a recession as severe as The Great Depression. Due to a decrease in investment, the Fed's interest rates were higher than the actual world's interest rate, which subsequently devalued the USD in comparison to international currencies. As a result, the US experienced a trade deficit in the 1970s and 1980s. In 1980, Ronald Reagan was elected based on his campaign that promised reform and change.

1980 Energy Crisis: Undeniably, the consecutive miscalculated policies undertaken by the US government led to the early 1980s recession, which is said to be the worst since The Great Depression. The Federal Reserve maintained a "stop and go" interest rate policy (the sudden increase and decrease in the Fed's interest rates); as a result, companies kept prices high due to the volatility of the money market, resulting in an inflation rate of 11.1%.

In 1979, President Jimmy Carter appointed Paul Volcker as chairman of the Federal Reserve, whose primary task was to stabilize inflation. The tightening monetary policies undertaken by Volcker caused unemployment to rise, however, what chiefly intensified the recession was the Iranian Revolution which caused oil prices to skyrocket. In 1980, oil prices peaked at an unadjusted price of $37.4/barrel and at an inflation—adjusted price of $111.3/barrel. It may be argued that the Fed's mission failed since the tightening policies were nullified due to high oil prices. It is also worth mentioning that the American citizens spent less and were extremely dissatisfied with their government, creating a confidence crisis.

Double Dip Recession: Energy Crisis Recession of 1981–1982: During the summer of 1980, the US economy experienced modest growth. However, in 1981, after overthrowing the US-backed Iranian government, the new populist regime started to cut oil exports, creating a third energy crisis and recession in the US. The term "Double Dip" best describes the situation, since the third energy crisis resulted in a second "dipped" recession in the US.

1981 Omnibus Budget Reconciliation Act: In response to the forecasted recession, the US Senate passed two bills known as Reagan's fiscal reform plan. These consisted of tax cuts, an increase in military funds and a reduction in domestic funds. In 1982, the Act did indeed help the US overcome the recession. It is also worth mentioning that Reagan got reelected in 1984 after the pseudo-success he experienced in 1982. According to Reagan, this set of policies would fix and reduce the Federal deficit, but it turned into a bubble that would burst at the end of 1986. The ballooning was caused by a slow growth in the production sector and the reduction in Federal revenues due to tax cuts. Consequently, the US experienced an increase in national debt, slow economic growth and consecutive budget deficits for two consecutive presidential terms.

Policy Analysis: The unprecedented recovery in 1982 remains a source of dispute among economists. Some argue that the increase in military spending stimulated the markets (the theory of "Military Keynesianism"). Others give credit to Reagan's tax cuts and the gradual loosening of the tight monetary policies used to stabilize inflation. Nonetheless, the recovery was uneven and unpredictable. It is also crucial to bear in mind that Reagan's bills created a huge build-up in national debt and increased the gap between the social classes. Moreover, the income of the working class was affected by inflation, whereas the wealthy got richer. The issue of whether Reagan favored macroeconomic welfare or the welfare of the people remains open for debate.

The United States' S&L Crisis (1986-1995)

By Antranik Artinian

What are S&Ls? Savings & Loans associations (S&Ls) are financial institutions which primarily focus on lending mortgages to prospective small homeowners. Initially, S&Ls were organized by small neighborhood residents that lacked financial capabilities to own their own homes. In the 1900s, banks were unable to give mortgages, leaving the floor open to financial innovation in the US. People in neighborhoods would pool their savings in the S&Ls and would get repaid when borrowers repay their mortgages. Generally, S&Ls are smaller than banks, but are extremely important for the liquidity of money and mortgage markets.

What Happened? Many regulatory and misled decision-making frameworks contributed to the crisis. In the 1980s, the status quo of S&Ls was one of insolvency and near bankruptcy. Consequently, the regulatory bodies under the Carter administration loosened restrictions on S&Ls and granted them permission to give out commercial and consumer loans with hopes of promoting the growth of these institutions. The US government started increasing the quantum of insurance deposits (i.e. even if S&Ls lost money, the government covered them with insurance for them to stay liquid). This created a state of moral hazard—the careless incentive of investing in riskier assets—since the depositors were clueless towards the risky investment opportunities that S&Ls undertook and to where the funds were channeled.

Further deregulation enacted by the Reagan administration intensified the hazardous situation. S&Ls were granted authorization to invest larger portions of earnings in real estate. Also, S&Ls were less subject to monetary control and were granted permission to invest in risky deals including junk bonds. Not only were depositors careless towards monitoring their investments, because of government support, but S&Ls were also willing to take much larger risks since they were insolvent. In fact, the regulations were intended to allow S&Ls to "grow" because of the Reagan administration's policies which discouraged real estate price inflation. Another regulation which was overlooked by the government was the use of looser accounting and auditing frameworks in reporting financial distress. S&Ls sought the opportunity of salvaging their losses by undertaking risky investments and unconsciously deceiving the financial structure in the US.

Ultimately, insolvent institutions cannot last for long and S&Ls felt their first disturbance when the Fed increased interest rates. As previously discussed, the 1980s was a decade characterized by high inflation rates, so the Fed increased interest rates to limit inflation. However, S&Ls' earnings were received with fixed interest rates, thus signaling losses in millions on their balance sheets. At this point, S&Ls were known to become Zombie institutions backed by the US government.

Zombie S&Ls. By definition, a zombie bank is an insolvent financial institution that operates under the implicit or explicit support of a third party or the government. As previously discussed, the insolvent S&Ls were leveraging their losses by pooling what was left of their liquid assets into risky investments. Not only did the losses in the mortgage market triple, but surprisingly, policymakers did not let go of the zombies. Some argue that the eradication of S&Ls would have created a banking crisis and mistrust in the economy, but that seems unlikely especially under the new G. Bush administration which instilled trust, reform and hope. Notwithstanding, these misguided and laissez-faire policies were the fruit of fraud and corrupt decision-makers.

Unfolding of the Crisis. Although the thrift industry experienced a 56% growth between 1982 and 1985 due to legislative changes, this growth was artificial and fueled by the government. After undertaking suicidal investment opportunities and leveraging losses, taxpayers and depositors ultimately paid the price of the S&Ls' fraud and hazardous actions.

Texas was the stage of a major recession, comprising more than half of S&Ls losses nationwide. As a result, in 1987, real estate prices plummeted and oil prices soared. In 1988, the peak year of the crisis, the government stopped channeling funds to S&Ls and let the zombies fail when losses tripled. By 1989, more than a 1000 S&Ls were doomed to fail.

Fraud & the Keating Five. It is worth mentioning some fraudulent and scandalous actions committed by five US senators during the

S&Ls crisis. This scandal represents, to this day, the greed of elected representatives and the vices of the American society. These five senators were accused of corruption with the Lincoln S&L along with its Chairman Charles Keating, Jr. After the institution's collapse in 1989, the federal government recorded a loss of $3 billion where more than 23,000 bondholders and investors saw their life savings disappear overnight. The investigation proved that Mr. Keating channeled $1.3 million in political donations to the Keating Five for their electoral campaigns.

Enforcement Act of 1989 & Recovery from the Crisis. In February, President George W. Bush unveiled the bail-out plan, and Congress passed the Financial Institutions Reform, Recovery and Enforcement Act of 1989. Reforms included the abolishment of the S&L regulator and therefore created a new body of regulation under the supervision of the Federal Deposit Insurance Corporation (FDIC) and the Office of Thrift Supervision. The Resolution Trust Corporation (RTC) was created to dissolve the remaining 747 insolvent S&Ls with assets worth over $407 billion. Eventually, the RTC closed on December 31, 1995, marking the end of the crisis and amounting to losses of approximately $124 billion to the government and taxpayers.

Policy analysis. Arguably, the aftermath of the S&Ls crisis contributed to the early 1990s recession. However, the Bush reforms paved the way to a period of profitability and stability for the American people, up until 2008. Also, it may be argued that the 2007 subprime mortgage crisis is a déjà vu of the S&Ls crisis. Indeed, the conditions and unfolding of events are quite similar, and this would mean that policymakers did not learn from their past mistakes. Thence, policies and reforms must be set in a way that prevents the re-insurgence of another financial crisis.

Black Monday (1987)

By Antranik Artinian

What Happened? Black Monday refers to the stock market crash that occurred on October 19, 1987, when the Dow Jones Index lost 22% of its value. Most economists and experts have speculated on the causes of the crash. According to several economic models, the crash came as an absurd reaction, making it shabby to explain among some economists.

Causes of the Crash. Financial crises never happen overnight. A series of events stacked up and generated panic, which in turn led to fire selling when the stock market opened. Due to the early 1980s recession, the US accumulated sovereign debt, accordingly, the US Secretary of Treasury, James Baker, designed a plan that would help reduce the alarming rise in the US trade deficit, requiring a devaluation of the US dollar. The devaluation would make American goods more competitive in the international market and would also encourage foreign investors to purchase US securities. However, Baker neglected the fact that the US stock market had not been corrected in the preceding five years, meaning that stock prices kept rising post-recession. Investors started feeling pessimistic, especially after noticing the standoff tensions between Kuwait and Iran, which would disrupt oil supplies and increase oil prices. Ultimately, on October 19, 1987, investors felt jittery and performed panic selling. Yet, what amplified the crisis was of technical essence and relied on the new setup of computerized and High Frequency Trading (HFT) algorithms. These algorithms are unmanned and follow a specific trend based on market forces. Hence, said series of events pushed prices downwards and the effect got amplified by the computerized algorithms selling millions of stocks on Black Monday.

Spillover Effect on Foreign Economies. Due to the newly installed computerized systems, the unified prices worldwide plummeted. The crash started in Hong Kong and then spread throughout Asia and Europe, rapidly reaching the US. Many countries were extremely affected, such as New Zealand, which underwent a deep recession during the following year. Nonetheless, other countries like Japan were able to rebound from the crisis in a few months.

Fed Reserve Intervention. During the following weeks, the Federal Reserve intervened, as a lender of last resort, by purchasing US securities in the open market with the aim to inject money, or simply to increase money supply. Other policies that focused on preventing the spread of the crisis to other sectors of the economy were undertaken. Overnight trading and scheduled trades became prominent methods to interact with investors in order to reinstall confidence in the markets.

Avoiding the Crisis. It is of utmost importance to understand that asymmetric information and pessimism in a trader's psychology may create a total meltdown in the financial markets. However, policymakers must focus on preventing panic selling by dampening the effect of pessimism and computerized algorithms. Other than market monitoring, circuit breakers—a system which halts High Frequency Trading if market indices plummet—were introduced as a guarantee.

Early 1990's Recession

By Antranik Artinian

Preface of the Recession: Reaganomics, the economic policies taken by President Ronald Reagan, precipitated an economic boom in the 1980s accompanied by a huge amount of debt and government deficit. The Reagan boom was artificial and unsustainable. These policies eventually played a role in the Black Monday Crash of 1987, albeit the events are considered to be economically independent. Furthermore, the recession was a parallel by-product of the S&Ls crisis, which contributed to the gradual decline of the economy. The American housing bubble left many Americans pessimistic and scared about their welfare. This pessimism and decrease in consumer confidence is referred to as "animal spirits".

Roots of the Recession: Due to the continuous governmental support for S&Ls and the greed of some policymakers, $124 billion were lost from the US economy in the S&Ls fraud scandal. In 1992, unemployment increased from 5% and peaked at 7.8%. This was essentially due to the cut in defense spending in an economy which was experiencing hardships. Furthermore, the downsizing of the defense workforce by 240,000 jobs may have contributed to the recession. Another major cause would be the tightening monetary policy undertaken by the Fed by increasing interest rates. The curbing of inflation by increasing interest rates came at the expense of a decrease in investments and a plummet in GDP. Also, North American exports weakened due to the economic recessions and complications in Europe and Japan, the US's and Canada's best trading partners. However, what really intensified the recession is of exogenous economic essence: Iraq's invasion of Kuwait.

Price of Oil: Controversially, the primary reason as to why the US and Canada experienced a recession is due to the sharp increase in oil prices, which slowed down the spending in the North American economy. On August 2, 1990, Iraqi troops occupied and annexed Kuwait after accusing the latter of taking their oil. Crude oil prices peaked at $20 a barrel, an unaccounted inflation which deeply affected consumption in America. In 1991, a US led international coalition entered Iraq to end Saddam Hussein's reign. Hussein used to be backed by the US, but after venturing into unprecedented territories (i.e. inflicting a recession on the US), his reign of terror needed to come to an end.

End of the Recession: Even though Bush gained popularity after the Persian Gulf War, he was accused of dragging the recession. Be that as it may, his 1992 reelection brought back consumer confidence and spending due to his famous pledge "read my lips: no new taxes". With the US acquiring Iraqi oil, a strong president and emerging victorious, the recession wore off.

The Wall Street Crash (1929) and The Great Depression (1929-1930)

By Antranik Artinian

Black Thursday: What Happened? A cold gloomy autumn day on Wall Street, a day full of fear and fright, October 24, 1929, signals the day that the largest stock exchange in the world began to crumble. This horrific day, labeled by many as "Black Thursday", embodies the downfall of capitalism. 12.9 million shares were traded in one day, creating panic among investors that intended to salvage their losses. Instead, this fear unleashed a financial meltdown in the upcoming days, giving way to a ten-year global depression. It has been reported that investment companies and major banks were able to sustain the crash by buying primary securities and maintaining prices, but this attempt did not last for long. The panic recommenced on October 28 (Black Monday) and continued on October 29 (Black Tuesday) with 16 million shares being traded and prices crashing by 40%. According to the Bureau of Labor Statistics (BLS), the United States' real Gross Domestic Product (GDP) halved due to deflation, unemployment rose from 3% to 25% and ultimately slowed global trade by spreading an economic depression throughout the rest of the world.

Black Thursday: Why did it happen? The 1920s was an effectively prosperous decade for the US; a decade of stable prices and few ongoing recessions. Post-World War I, technological innovation pushed companies to pioneer and cater for demand, creating a rise in stock prices of major and subset companies. However, under the Hoover administration, the US government wanted to limit the stock market's expansion. In the spring of 1928, via the use of monetary instruments, the Federal Reserve System (Fed) gradually raised their funds rate and kept raising them during the recession that started in August 1929.

Both the political and economic conditions of the time led to an orchestrated banking crisis in 1929. The death of the Federal Bank's governor Benjamin Strong created a power vacuum and left monetary regulations in the hands of less sensible regulators. Also, it is worth mentioning that the US banking system was already in a preamble crisis. The increase in the prices of agricultural goods during World War I encouraged American farmers to take out loans and expand their businesses. American farmers were not able to repay their debt due to the plunge in the prices of agricultural commodities post-World War I. Banks subsequently faced liquidity problems, leading to a meltdown and mistrust in the banking industry. The Fed did not increase the supply of money to combat deflation and did not decrease reserve requirements, staying numb to the banks' plight. The failure of banks created more panic and depositors rushed to take out their bank's savings in order to hide them under their mattresses and carpets.

The Global Depression. In response to the banking crisis, the Fed regulators maintained a low money supply to preserve the United States' gold standard and to protect the national currency from depreciation. By definition, the gold standard would set the value of a nation's currency, and it was the Central Banks' responsibility to undertake monetary actions to preserve the currency's value. In response to the banking panic, the Fed maintained a tight monetary policy, fearing that foreigners would have lost confidence in the gold standard. Furthermore, since the USD was pegged to the gold's price, the lack of trust in the gold standard would have created a currency crisis and subsequent large gold outflows from the US. Alongside the Fed's tightening, the panic led to investors turning into safer trusted currency markets while maintaining the gold standard.

A key factor that remains unexplained relates to how the crisis spread to the rest of the world. Due to the high deflation in the US and high post-War inflation in Europe, American products and securities became desirable for foreign investments, so this increased gold inflow to the US. Governments around the world adopted contractionary monetary policies by raising interest rates to limit gold outflow. Nonetheless, the rise in the interest rates slowed down international trade, causing the bankruptcy of many major companies. Also, high inflation rates (commonly known as hyperinflation) prevailed in post-war havocked countries such as Germany due to the printing of money and the loss of the gold standard.

Life During the Depression: At the lowest point of the Great Depression, unemployment soared to 25% in the US workforce. The fortunate few who still had jobs saw a cut in their wages and savings, and even saw their hours reduced to part-time. The upper-middle class, self-employed doctors and lawyers had their income nearly halved. The financial burden eventually created familial and psychological problems. The national suicide and divorce filing rates rose to an all-time high in 1933.

The aforementioned scenario repeated itself in almost every nation on the globe, however, the situation in Germany had an inhumane and catastrophic turn. German officials were forced to print money to satisfy import requirements, leading to a phenomenon of hyperinflation in prices. Studies have shown that one-third of the German workforce in 1933 were unemployed, creating a state of social desolation.

Political Movements and Social Change: The US witnessed an era of political innovation under the Roosevelt administration. Roosevelt inherited and enacted reforms in a state plunged in poverty, unemployment and economic disintegration. Under Roosevelt's New Deal reform plan, the US focused entirely on the American people and their living standards, which required government intervention in most economic and political processes. This was also the time when Marxism started to flourish in America and the world, enacting a brain-tease in the capitalist mindset. Marxist movements idealized the concept of equality and a better life in the Soviet Union. Meanwhile, Adolf Hitler and Benito Mussolini were gaining power by building their fascist empires. The social and economic hostility pushed the Germans and the Italians to elect totalitarian regimes to save them from their ongoing misery.

How did the Great Depression End? The Great Depression ended with the Japanese attack on Pearl Harbor and a declaration of war. The US shifted its economic resources toward military deployment and nuclear research. The newly funded military contracts provided millions of jobs and an increase in both government intervention and wages. With an increase in government spending and national military output, trust was reinstalled in the US government and its institutions, ending a ten-year global depression. As most economists would say, the market cleared itself. Ironically, a world war ended an economic collapse.

The Dot-Com Bubble (2000-2002)

By Antranik Artinian

Defining Dot-com companies: In 1993, the release of the very first web browser, Mosaic, helped the popularization of the World Wide Web (WWW). As of 1997, 35% of US households owned computers and were surfing the World Wide Web, pinpointing the start of the Information Age. Hence, the 1990s was a period of economic boom and technological innovation. The low interest rates increased capital availability and bolstered the formation of Dot-com (or Internet) companies. The Telecommunication Act of 1996 boosted the prestige of forming Dot-com companies and the incentive of making tremendous profits. The investing wave was so powerful and tempting that people started quitting their jobs to become techpreneurs.

Inflating the Bubble: A price bubble in economics refers to the artificial, unhealthy increase in prices that would eventually "burst" or massively depreciate in value once an unprecedented event occurs. This artificial increase in stock prices of Dot-com companies was coupled by fad-based investing due to the abundance of venture funding for startups and the failure of Dot-com companies in managing their profits and spending. Until 1999, hundreds of companies were receiving immediate responses from their investors and became active in uncalculated spending. Furthermore, these companies wasted millions of dollars in marketing with the incentive of increasing market share. Also, investors only took into account the increase in sale volumes as an indicator for their investments. Dot-com companies eventually adopted a "grow big or go home", "grow at any cost" and "growth over profits" tactics. The NASDAQ (a stock index that represents all the companies traded on the NASDAQ stock exchange) experienced a 400% (5-fold) rise between 1995 and 2000. It is also worth mentioning that the media played a huge role in luring in investors by exploiting the public's interest in the new technology.

How did the Bubble Burst? The US government began reducing interest rates to limit inflation, and this created a more volatile market due to the debate on whether Dot-com companies would be better off if they borrowed money. On March 10th, 2000, the NASDAQ index peaked and lost massive value, nullifying most of the profits made since the bubble started. A week later, the Japanese government announced that it had entered a recession. Generally speaking, a recession in a developed country like Japan signals red flags for investors, who eventually will start selling shares. By 2001, over $1 trillion was lost, thence, the "grow big or go home" strategy doomed the tech industry. The bubble eventually burst.

Survival: Countless tech companies declared bankruptcy such as Pets.co, 360Networks, eToys, etc. Nonetheless, few internet-based companies were able to withstand the losses due to their liquid capital—namely Microsoft, Amazon, eBay and Cisco. Hence, investors and people in general must learn to question their investments instead of riding the wave. It is of utmost importance to understand that short-term artificial investments may lead to bubbles that will eventually burst. A more recent example that illustrates that investors have not learned from their past is Gamestop. In short, diligence and self-control are necessary qualities, not only to become a successful investor, but for the greater good of the economy.

9/11 and its Economic Repercussions (2001-Present)

By Antranik Artinian

What happened? On September 11, 2001, Al-Qaeda's terrorists hijacked four planes heading towards the West coast. The intended targets were economic centers in order to cripple the US economy: Wall Street, the Pentagon and the White House. The first two airplanes hit their targets: Tower One of the World Trade Center collapsed at 8:46 a.m. and Tower Two at 9:03 a.m. The third plane crashed into the Pentagon at 9:37 a.m. Fortunately, the fourth plane never hit its target, the White House, after some brave passengers attacked the terrorists and forcefully crashed the airplane into a field in Sharpsville, Pennsylvania at 10:03 a.m.

Cost of the Damages. The total death toll amounted to 2,977—not including the 19 hijackers. 9/11 cost the United States $55 billion. Prospective passengers were both terrorized and afraid of flying, which cost the airline industry $5 billion during the following year. Insurance companies lost around $32 billion before signing the Terrorism Risk Insurance Act of 2002, which required the government to pay for 90% of the losses. Not to mention financial institutions suffered drastically, including Wall Street which closed for four consecutive days.

War on Terror and Debt Crisis. The War on Terror, launched by President George W. Bush as a response to 9/11, is a military campaign that includes the Afghan War and the Iraqi War. The US attacked the Taliban who were responsible for hiding Osama bin Laden, Al-Qaeda's feared leader, who then escaped to Pakistan. In 2001, President Bush spent around $22.9 billion as an immediate military response to 9/11, however, since 2001, US presidents Bush, Obama, and Trump spent a cumulative amount of $6 trillion on this military campaign. The most significant impact of 9/11 would be the US long-run debt crisis. The $6 trillion spent on defense and military were allocated from debt, increasing the US debt substantially and amounting to $26 trillion in 2021.

2001 Recession. As previously discussed, the 2001 Recession was stimulated by the Dot-com bubble and the failure of mainstream tech investing. Regardless, 9/11 was an additional factor that worsened the recession. Wall Street closed for four consecutive days to prevent fire selling and further devaluation in stock value. The economy contracted by 1.7% after the attacks, prolonging the recession and rebounding in 2002.

Policy Analysis. Whether defense spending is too high and would be better allocated to the American people in the form of healthcare and transfer payments remains controversial. People may argue that 9/11 is a tragedy that must be avoided by fighting back. Others acknowledge the aforementioned claim, but argue that $6 trillion in debt is not worth it and harmful to the US economy and subsequently to Americans. What remains shocking is that after twenty years, the stigma of defense spending has not changed.

Bibliography

AFRICA
"Jasmine Revolution". 2021. *Encyclopædia Britannica*.

https://www.britannica.com/event/Jasmine-Revolution

"Egypt Uprising of 2011". 2021. Britannica.
https://www.britannica.com/event/Egypt-Uprising-of-2011

"Arab Spring". 2021. *Encyclopædia Britannica*.
https://www.britannica.com/event/Arab-Spring

"Libya Revolt of 2011". 2021. *Encyclopædia Britannica*.
https://www.britannica.com/event/Libya-Revolt-of-2011

Erin Blakemore. 2019. "What was the Arab Spring and how did it spread?". *National Geographic*.
https://www.nationalgeographic.com/culture/article/arab-spring-cause

George Joffé. 2011. "The Arab Spring in North Africa: Origins and Prospects". University of Cambridge.

"Arab Spring". 2020. History.
https://www.history.com/topics/middle-east/arab-spring

Kali Robinson. 2020. "The Arab Spring at Ten Years: What's the Legacy of the Uprisings?". Council on Foreign Relations.
https://www.cfr.org/article/arab-spring-ten-years-whats-legacy-uprisings

Samuel Momodu. 2018. "Second Sudanese Civil War (1983-2005)". *Black Past*.
https://www.blackpast.org/global-african-history/events-global-african-history/second-sudanese-civil-war-1983-2005/

Frontline World. 2005. "Sudan: Fracs & Stats". *PBS*.
https://www.pbs.org/frontlineworld/stories/sudan/facts.html

"South Sudan country profile". 2018. *BBC*.
https://www.bbc.com/news/world-africa-14069082

"South Sudan". 2021. Human Rights Watch.
https://www.hrw.org/africa/south-sudan

"South Sudan". 2021. CIA.
https://www.cia.gov/the-world-factbook/countries/south-sudan/#military-and-security

"Sudan Fact Sheet". 2018. *Jewish World Watch*. http://www.jww.org/wp-content/uploads/2018/01/FactSheet-Sudan-Winter2018.pdf

"Sudanese civil war". 2020. New World Encyclopedia. https://www.newworldencyclopedia.org/entry/Sudanese_civil_war

"Sudan: 1985-2005". 2015. *Tufts*. https://sites.tufts.edu/atrocityendings/2015/08/07/sudan-2nd-civil-war-darfur/

Norimitsu Onishi. 2021. "France Has 'Overwhelming' Responsibility for Rwanda Genocide, Report Says". The New York Times. https://www.nytimes.com/2021/03/26/world/europe/france-rwanda-genocide.html

"France was 'blind' to Rwanda genocide, French report says". 2021. BBC News. https://www.bbc.com/news/world-europe-56536659

"Rwandan Genocide". 2019. History.com. https://www.history.com/topics/africa/rwandan-genocide

"The Rwandan Genocide". United to End Genocide. http://endgenocide.org/learn/past-genocides/the-rwandan-genocide/

"Rwandan genocide"100 days of slaughter". 2019. BBC News. https://www.bbc.com/news/world-africa-26875506

"Rwandan Genocide". 2021. World Without Genocide. http://worldwithoutgenocide.org/genocides-and-conflicts/rwandan-genocide

"A history of Apartheid in South Africa". 2019. South African History. https://www.sahistory.org.za/article/history-apartheid-south-africa

"Apartheid". 2020. History.com. https://www.history.com/topics/africa/apartheid

Erin Blakemore. 2019. "The Harsh Reality of Life Under Apartheid in South Africa". History.com. https://www.history.com/news/apartheid-policies-photos-nelson-mandela

Erin Blakemore. 2020. "How Nelson Mandela fought apartheid - and why his work is not complete". National Geographic.

https://www.nationalgeographic.com/history/article/nelson-mandela-fought-apartheid-work-not-complete

Adedokun, Ademola, Kamoru, Ramat Toyin Kamorudeen and Ayodeji Oluwadare Olarinmoye. "Ebola outbreak in West Africa, 2014-2016: Epidemic timeline, differential diagnoses, determining factors, and lessons for future response". Journal of Infection and Public Health. 2020.

https://www.sciencedirect.com/science/article/pii/S1876034120304275Obinna O

Akpalu, Albert, Matthew Foster, Mairi McConnochie, M Mourtalla Ka, Oleribe , Babatunde L Salako, Simon D Taylor-Robinson. "Ebola virus disease epidemic in West Africa: lessons learned and issues arising from West African countries". Clin Med. 2015.

https://www.ncbi.nlm.nih.gov/pmc/articles/PMC4954525/

"2014-2016 Ebola Outbreak in West Africa". CDC.

https://www.cdc.gov/vhf/ebola/history/2014-2016-outbreak/index.html

David Peters. 2017. "The Ebola epidemic in Liberia: the role of communities and local leadership in overcoming catastrophe and building health system resilience". European Journal of Public Health.

https://academic.oup.com/eurpub/article/27/suppl_3/ckx187.588/4556554

Christopher Hitchens. 2006. A Chronology of the Algerian War of Independence. The Atlantic.

https://www.theatlantic.com/magazine/archive/2006/11/a-chronology-of-the-algerian-war-of-independence/305277/4/

"Algeria: War of independence". 2015. World Peace Foundation.

https://sites.tufts.edu/atrocityendings/2015/08/07/algeria-war-of-independence/

"Algeria". *Encyclopædia Britannica*.

https://www.britannica.com/place/Algeria/Nationalist-movements

"The Angolan Civil War (1975-2002): A Brief History". South African History Online.

https://www.sahistory.org.za/article/angolan-civil-war-1975-2002-brief-history

Ben Rosie. The Angolan Civil War: Conflict Economics or the Divine Right of Kings? E-International Relations. 2020.
https://www.e-ir.info/2020/12/02/the-angolan-civil-war-conflict-economics-or-the-divine-right-of-kings/

Encyclopædia Britannica. Angola in the 21st century.
https://www.britannica.com/place/Angola/Angola-in-the-21st-century

David Cook. 2011. The Rise of Boko Haram in Nigeria. Combating Terrorism Center.
https://ctc.usma.edu/the-rise-of-boko-haram-in-nigeria/

Policy & Practice Brief. Nigeria's Boko Haram. Accord.
https://www.accord.org.za/publication/nigerias-boko-haram/

"Boko Haram: Nigerian Islamic group". *Encyclopædia Britannica*.
https://www.britannica.com/topic/Boko-Haram

John Campbell. 2014. "Boko Haram: origins, challenges and responses". Norwegian Peacebuilding Resource Centre.
https://www.files.ethz.ch/isn/184795/5cf0ebc94fb36d66309681cda24664f9.pdf

"Boko Haram in Nigeria". Council on Foreign Relations.
https://www.cfr.org/global-conflict-tracker/conflict/boko-haram-nigeria

ASIA

"About Myanmar." 2012. UNDP in Myanmar.
https://www.mm.undp.org/content/myanmar/en/home/countryinfo.html.

"China's Great Leap Forward - Association for Asian Studies." 2020. Association for Asian Studies. July 13, 2020.
https://www.asianstudies.org/publications/eaa/archives/chinas-great-leap-forward/.

"First Five Year Plan (1953-1957)." 2021. Chineseposters.net.
https://chineseposters.net/themes/first-five-year-plan.

"Great Leap Forward | Definition, Facts, & Significance | Britannica." 2021. *Encyclopædia Britannica.* https://www.britannica.com/event/Great-Leap-Forward.

"Korean War | Combatants, Summary, Years, Map, Casualties, & Facts | Britannica." 2021. *Encyclopædia Britannica.* https://www.britannica.com/event/Korean-War.

"Pelosi Statement on Hong Kong Protests and Extradition Bill." 2019. Speaker Nancy Pelosi. June 11, 2019. https://www.speaker.gov/newsroom/61119-2.

"Vietnam War | Facts, Summary, Years, Timeline, Casualties, Combatants, & Facts | Britannica." 2021. *Encyclopædia Britannica.* https://www.britannica.com/event/Vietnam-War.

"Why the United States Went to War in Vietnam - Foreign Policy Research Institute." 2019. Foreign Policy Research Institute. https://www.fpri.org/article/2017/04/united-states-went-war-vietnam/.

Cucchisi, Jennifer. 2002. "The Causes and Effects of the Chinese Civil War, 1927-1949.".https://scholarship.shu.edu/cgi/viewcontent.cgi?article=3416&context=dissertations.

Dudziak, Mary. 2019. "The Toxic Legacy of the Korean War." Washington Post. The Washington Post. March 2019. https://www.washingtonpost.com/outlook/2019/03/01/toxic-legacy-korean-war/.

Moreno, Ramon. 1997. "Lessons from Thailand." Federal Reserve Bank of San Francisco. Federal Reserve Bank of San Francisco. November 7, 1997. https://www.frbsf.org/economic-research/publications/economic-letter/1997/november/lessons-from-thailand/.

Morrison, Allen. 2019. "How Hong Kong's Protests Are Affecting Its Economy." The Conversation. August 22, 2019. https://theconversation.com/how-hong-kongs-protests-are-affecting-its-economy-122098.

National Library Board, Singapore. 2021. "Economic Survey of Singapore." Nlb.gov.sg. 2021.
https://eservice.nlb.gov.sg/item_holding.aspx?bid=4082216.
Radio Free Asia. 2015. "The 10th Anniversary of Myanmar's Saffron Revolution: A Look Back." Rfa.org. 2015.
https://www.rfa.org/english/news/special/saffron/.
The Independent. 2011. "Burma: Inside the Saffron Revolution," September 17, 2011.
https://www.independent.co.uk/news/world/asia/burma-inside-the-saffron-revolution-5329400.html.
Yu, Verna, and Lily Kuo. 2019. "Hong Kong: 1.7m People Defy Police to March in Pouring Rain." The Guardian. The Guardian. August 18, 2019.
https://www.theguardian.com/world/2019/aug/18/hong-kong-huge-rally-china-condemns-us-gross-interference.

EUROPE

"First Sino-Japanese War". 2020. Encyclopedia Britannica.
https://www.britannica.com/event/First-Sino-Japanese-War-1894-1895
"Meiji Restoration". 2020. Encyclopedia Britannica.
https://www.britannica.com/event/Meiji-Restoration
"Russo-Japanese War". 2021. Encyclopedia Britannica.
https://www.britannica.com/event/Russo-Japanese-War
"U.K. Votes to leave the E.U". 2016. BBC News, Retrieved from:
https://www.bbc.co.uk/news/politics/eu_referendum/results
"U.K. Results: Conservative win majority". 2019. Retrieved from:
https://www.bbc.co.uk/news/election/2019/results
Bloomberg, (2020) China Turns to Lobsters, Wine and Coal to 'Punish' Australia, Bloomberg News, Retrieved from:
https://www.bloomberg.com/news/articles/2020-11-03/china-turns-to-lobsters-wine-and-coal-to-punish-australia
"How Huawei Landed at the Center of Global Tech Tussle". 2021. Bloomberg News, Retrieved from

British Cabinet office (2015) National Security Strategy and Strategic Defence and Security Review 2015, British Government, Retrieved from:
https://www.gov.uk/government/publications/national-security-strategy-and-strategic-defence-and-security-review-2015
"Global Britain in a Competitive Age: the Integrated Review of Security, Defence, Development and Foreign Policy, British Government". 2021. Retrieved from:
https://www.gov.uk/government/publications/global-britain-in-a-competitive-age-the-integrated-review-of-security-defence-development-and-foreign-policy
Chutter. A. 2021. "Here's why Britain is struggling to form a fully effective carrier strike group". defence news, retrieved from:
https://www.defensenews.com/naval/2020/06/26/heres-why-britain-is-struggling-to-form-a-fully-effective-carrier-strike-group/
Grevatt, J. 2021. UK Integrated Review affirms 'tilt' to Asia-Pacific, Janes, Retrieved from:
https://www.janes.com/defence-news/news-detail/uk-integrated-review-affirms-tilt-to-asia-pacific_16278
Greve, Andrew Q, & Levy, Jack S. 2018. "Power Transitions, Status Dissatisfaction, and War: The Sino-Japanese War of 1894-1895". Security Studies, 27(1), 148-178.
Lawson. E & Barrons. R. 2016. "Warfare in the Information Age". The RUSI Journal, 161:5, 20-26, DOI: 10.1080/03071847.2016.1253371 Retrieved from:
https://www.tandfonline.com/action/showCitFormats?doi=10.1080%2F03071847.2016.1253371
Mehdian-Staffell. S. 2021. "The Integrated Review: A Technological Revolution at the Heart of UK Defence and National Security". RUSI, retrieved from:
https://rusi.org/explore-our-research/publications/commentary/integrated-review-technological-revolution-heart-uk-defence-and-national-security

Raab, D. 2020. "Dominic Raab MP tells MPs of plans for a 'Global Britain'", U.K. Parliament, Retrieved from:
https://www.parliament.uk/business/news/2020/february/statement-on-global-britain/
State Department, (n.d.) "The Treaty of Portsmouth, History of the State Department", Retrieved from:
https://history.state.gov/milestones/1899-1913/portsmouth-treaty
Yun, Ji-won. 2020. "The Origin of Territorial Disputes in Northeast Asia and Japanese Perceptions of the Russo-Japanese War: A Literature Review". Pacific Focus, 35(1), 59-75.

LATIN AMERICA AND THE CARIBBEAN

"Chicago Boys - Memoria Chilena, Biblioteca Nacional De Chile". 2021. *Memoriachilena.Gob.Cl.* Retrieved from:
http://www.memoriachilena.gob.cl/602/w3-article-98015.html.
"Cómo cayó Batista" pp. 87-85 en La revolución cubana. México: El Colegio de México, 2015.
"Cuba Libre: La forja de héroes". 2017. Código Rojo1917.
https://www.youtube.com/watch?v=tLKJLlA_U9w&list=PLpVP6wt-Z3Z18WDefGdIYLIAeIfNhdHF&
"Década perdida: entenda o que aconteceu na América Latina nos anos 80!". 2021. *Politize!.* Retrieved from:
https://www.politize.com.br/decada-perdida-e-america-latina/
"Dictadura Militar no Brasil". 2021. . *Politize!.* Retrieved from:
https://www.politize.com.br/ditadura-militar-no-brasil/
"Jânio Quadros-Real motivo de Renúncia". 2018. Creusa Nacimiento.
https://www.youtube.com/watch?v=zwnwLBQD81A
"Los años más oscuros de Chile". 2019. *La Vanguardia.* Retrieved from:
https://www.lavanguardia.com/vida/junior-report/20191108/471450047349/dictadura-chile-augusto-pinochet-represion.html
"On Poor Relations and the Nouveau Riche: Shining Path and the Radical Peruvian Left". in Steve Stern ed. Shining and Other Paths: War and Society in Peru, 1980-1995. Durham: Duke University Press, pp. 60 - 83. 136-.157, Latin American Research Review, XLIV, 2, 2009.
"Personajes de la revolución mexicana". Mexicana: Repositorio del patrimonio cultural de México. Retrieved from:
https://mexicana.cultura.gob.mx/es/repositorio/x2abesp3qm-1

"Venezuela crisis: Facts, FAQs and how to help". 2020. *Worldvision.* Retrieved from: https://www.worldvision.org/disaster-relief-news-stories/venezuela-crisis-facts

Arce, Moisés. 2005. Market Reform in Society, Post-Crisis Politics and Economic Change in Authoritarian Peru. The Pennsylvania State University Press: University Park, PA. Chapter 2.

Ávila, Felipe y Pedro Salmerón. Cap I "Por qué hubo en México una revolución" y Cap. IV "La

Burt, Jo-Marie. 2006. Contesting the Terrain of Politics: State-Society Relation in Urban Peru, 1950-2000. In Paul Drake and Erick Hershberg eds. State and Society in Conflict, University of Pittsburgh Press, pp. 220-256. Colegio de México, 2014.

Concha Monardes, Raúl. 2014. "Chile: neoliberalismo y subdesarrollo económico" pp.25-42 en CUHSO. Cultura-Hombre-Sociedad, XXIV, 2. Retrieved from: https://cuhso.uct.cl/index.php/cuhso/article/view/870/770

Coppola, Frances. 2018. "Why Venezuela's Hyperinflation Problem Is so Difficult to Solve." *Forbes.* December 31, 2018. Retrieved from: https://www.forbes.com/sites/francescoppola/2018/12/31/why-venezuelas-hyperinflation-problem-is-so-difficult-to-solve/?sh=4a673b3b373c.

Documental, "La historia de Cuba Libre" cap. 5,

Documental: "La Revolución mexicana" en https://www.youtube.com/watch?v=qH0tLz28hr8

Errázuriz, Luis Hernán. "Dictadura militar en Chile. Antecedentes del golpe estético-cultural" pp.

Fernandez Corugedo, Emilio and Jaime Guajardo. 2019. "Para os vizinhos de Venezuela, a migracão em massa traz custos e beneficios econômicos". International Monetary Funds. Retrieved from: https://www.imf.org/pt/News/Articles/2019/11/21/blog-for-venezuelas-neighbors-mass-migration-brings-economic-costs-and-benefits

Garciadiego, Javier "El porfiriato (1876-1911)" en Gisela von Wobeser (coord.) Historia de México.

Geografía e Historia. "Capítulo 12: "Años peronistas". 2013. Retrieved from: https://www.youtube.com/watch?v=5tNVgcsHBNg

Katz, Friedrich. De Díaz a Madero. Orígenes y estallido de la Revolución Mexicana. México: Era,

Knight, Alan. La Revolución Mexicana. México: Fondo de Cultura Económica, 2010

La izquierda latinoamericana a comienzos del siglo XXI: nuevas realidades y urgentes desafíos. Atilio A. Boron http://bibliotecavirtual.clacso.org.ar/clacso/osal/20110307010337/4ACBoron.pdf

México: SEP, FCE, 2010.

Montes, Rocio. 2020. "Richard Nixon: "Si Hay Una Forma De Desbancar A Allende, Mejor Hazlo"". *El País*. Retrieved from: https://elpais.com/internacional/2020-11-11/richard-nixon-si-hay-una-forma-de-desbancar-a-allende-mejor-hazlo.html.

Reid, Kathryn. 2020. "Venezuela Crisis: Facts, FAQs, and How to Help | World Vision." World Vision. June 23, 2020.

revolución popular" en Breve historia de la Revolución mexicana. México: Crítica, 2017.

Rojas, R. 2018 "The Latin American Left's Shifting Tides" Catalyst 2 (2)

Rojas, Rafael. "El antiguo régimen" pp. 19-24; "La dictadura", pp. 25-32, "Insurrección" pp. 59-70 y

Rojas, Rafael. 2015."El antiguo régimen" pp. 19-24; "La dictadura", pp. 25-32, "Insurrección" pp. 59-70 y "Cómo cayó Batista" pp. 87-85 en La revolución cubana. México: El Colegio de México.

Salvo Salazar, Manuel."Cómo se intalos el modelo de los Chicago boys en los primeros años de la dictadura". 2020. *Interferencia*. Retrieved from: https://interferencia.cl/articulos/como-se-instalo-el-modelo-de-los-chicago-boys-en-los-primeros-anos-de-la-dictadura

Sanz, Beatriz. "O lado obsucro do 'milagre econômico da dictadura: o boom da desigualdade'". 2017. *El País*. Retrieved from: https://brasil.elpais.com/brasil/2017/09/29/economia/1506721812_344807.html

Secretaría de Gobernación. 2018. "Revolción Mexicana, el gran movimiento social del Siglo XX". Gobierno de México. 2018. Retrieved from: https://www.gob.mx/segob/es/articulos/revolucion-mexicana-el-gran-movimiento-social-del-siglo-xx?idiom=es

Vergara Alberto (2014). "The Fujimori Regime through Tocqueville's Lens: Centralism, Regime Change, and Peripheral Elites in Contemporary Peru" in Paulo Drinot ed. Peru in Theory, pp, 19-47.

Zanatta, Loris. 2014."El peronismo" pp. 273-303 en Pablo Yankelevich (Coord.), Argentina. México: El Colegio de México.

MIDDLE EAST

"Sykes-Picot agreement". (n.d.). Encyclopædia Britannica. Retrieved April 22, 2021, from
https://www.britannica.com/event/Sykes-Picot-Agreement
Britain and france conclude Sykes-Picot agreement. (2009, October 28). Retrieved April 22, 2021, from
https://www.history.com/this-day-in-history/britain-and-france-conclude-sykes-picot-agreement
Shaw, S., & Shaw, E. (n.d.). The Turkish war for INDEPENDENCE, 1918–1923 (Chapter 5) - history of the Ottoman Empire and Modern Turkey. Retrieved April 22, 2021, from
https://www.cambridge.org/core/books/history-of-the-ottoman-empire-and-modern-turkey/turkish-war-for-independence-19181923/33BB1382FE0629F4F3F8F471AD562870
Druze revolt. (n.d.). Encyclopædia Britannica. Retrieved April 22, 2021, from https://www.britannica.com/event/Druze-revolt
"Military History: The Middle East in World War II". 2020. Retrieved April 24, 2021, from
https://www.thegreatcoursesdaily.com/the-middle-east-in-world-war-ii/
(www.dw.com), D. (n.d.). How Nazis courted the Islamic world during Wwii: Dw: 13.11.2017. Retrieved April 24, 2021, from
https://www.dw.com/en/how-nazis-courted-the-islamic-world-during-wwii/a-41358387
"Arab Israel War". (n.d.). Retrieved April 27, 2021, from
https://history.state.gov/milestones/1945-1952/arab-israeli-war
Rai, S. 2021. What were the causes and consequences of the 1948 Arab-Israeli War? Retrieved April 27, 2021, from
https://www.e-ir.info/2014/01/15/what-were-the-causes-and-consequences-of-the-1948-arab-israeli-war-2/
"Who are the Kurds?". 2019. Retrieved April 27, 2021, from
https://www.bbc.com/news/world-middle-east-29702440
The Kurdish CONFLICT. (n.d.). Retrieved April 27, 2021, from
https://www.britannica.com/place/Turkey/The-Kurdish-conflict
https://youtu.be/8w4Ku6l7OEI

Encyclopædia Britannica
https://www.britannica.com/event/Iranian-Revolution
http://www-personal.umich.edu/~rraham/black_friday.html
https://www.brookings.edu/blog/order-from-chaos/2019/01/24/the-iranian-revolution-a-timeline-of-events/

Taylor, A. (2016, January 14). Operation Desert Storm: 25 years since the first Gulf War. Retrieved April 30, 2021, from https://www.theatlantic.com/photo/2016/01/operation-desert-storm-25-years-since-the-first-gulf-war/424191/

Jazeera, A. (n.d.). The price of oslo - palestineremix. Retrieved April 30, 2021, from https://interactive.aljazeera.com/aje/palestineremix/the-price-of-oslo.html#/14

History.com Editors. (2018, February 16). Oslo accords. Retrieved April 30, 2021, from https://www.history.com/topics/middle-east/oslo-accords

Damon, A. (2021, March 15). We tell SYRIA'S human stories so that the 'victors' don't write its history. Retrieved May 05, 2021, from https://edition.cnn.com/2021/03/15/middleeast/syria-anniversary-damon-analysis-intl/index.html

Syria timeline: Since the uprising AGAINST ASSAD. (2021, March 12). Retrieved May 05, 2021, from https://www.usip.org/syria-timeline-uprising-against-assad

Jenkins, B. (2016, May 02). Five years after the death of Osama bin Laden, is the world safer? Retrieved May 07, 2021, from https://www.rand.org/blog/2016/05/five-years-after-the-death-of-osama-bin-laden-is-the.html

Corbin, J. (2015, June 17). Have we been told the truth about Bin Laden's death? Retrieved May 07, 2021, from https://www.bbc.com/news/world-middle-east-33152315

Jamal Khashoggi: All you need to know about Saudi JOURNALIST'S DEATH. (2021, February 24). Retrieved May 27, 2021, from https://www.bbc.com/news/world-europe-45812399

Myre, G., Kennedy, M., & Romo, V. (2021, February 26). U.S. Intelligence: Saudi Crown Prince Approved operation to KILL JAMAL KHASHOGGI. Retrieved May 27, 2021, from https://www.npr.org/2021/02/25/971215788/biden-administration-poised-to-release-report-on-killing-of-jamal-khashoggi

NORTH AMERICA

Frum, D. 2000. How we got here: The 70's: The decade that brought you modern life (for better or worse) (1st ed.). New York, NY: Basic Books.

World Bank, GDP growth (Annual%)—United States (n.d.), Retrieved from:
https://data.worldbank.org/indicator/NY.GDP.MKTP.KD.ZG?end=1991&locations=US&start=1961

Tran, M. 2009. "The 1979 Iranian Revolution and how the Guardian covered it". The Guardian, Retrieved from:
https://www.theguardian.com/news/blog/2009/feb/03/iranian-revolution-archive

Carter, J. 1979. Energy and National Goals-A Crisis of Confidence. Retrieved from:
https://www.americanrhetoric.com/speeches/jimmycartercrisisofconfidence.htm

"In pictures Iranian hostage crisis". 1979. BBC. Retrieved from:
http://news.bbc.co.uk/2/shared/spl/hi/picture_gallery/04/middle_east_iran_hostage_crisis/html/1.stm

Afghanistan Profile-Timeline. 2019. BBC. Retrieved from
https://www.bbc.com/news/world-south-asia-12024253

Reagan, R. 1980. Reagan 1980 Campaign Commercials, C-SPAN, Retrieved from:
https://www.c-span.org/video/?31280-1/reagan-1980-campaign-commercials

Cannon, L. 1980. Reagan:' Peace Through Strength'. The Washington Post. Retrieved from
https://www.washingtonpost.com/archive/politics/1980/08/19/reagan-peace-through-strength/f343ddc5-fbda-49fc-a524-6fbc29dfb312/

Reagan, R. 1983. 'Evil Empire' Retrieved from:
https://www.youtube.com/watch?v=FcSm-KAEFFA

Executive Office of the President of the United States, Historical Table- Budget of the United States Government. 2013. p. 193, Retrieved from: https://web.archive.org/web/20120417053737/http://www.whitehouse.gov/sites/default/files/omb/budget/fy2013/assets/hist.pdf

Pipes, R. 1981. U.S.-Soviet relations in the era of detente: Tragedy of errors. Boulder, Co.: Westview Press.

Chernoff, F. 1991. Ending the Cold War: The Soviet Retreat and the US Military Build-up. International Affairs (Royal Institute of International Affairs 1944-), 67(1), 111-126. doi:10.2307/2621222

Busch, A. 1997. Ronald Reagan and the Defeat of the Soviet Empire. Presidential Studies Quarterly, 27(3), 451-466. Retrieved May 12, 2020, from www.jstor.org/stable/27551762

"The Dance of the Euromissiles". 1983. The New York Times. Retrieved from https://www.nytimes.com/1983/11/07/opinion/the-dance-of-the-euromissiles.html

The Atomic Heritage Foundation. 2018. Strategic Defence Initiative (SDI), Retrieved from https://www.atomicheritage.org/history/strategic-defense-initiative-sdi

The White House. 1981. National Security Decision Directive (NSDD) 12, Retrieved from: https://catalog.archives.gov/id/6879613

Fischer, B. 2010. US foreign policy under Reagan and Bush. In M. Leffler & O. Westad (Eds.), The Cambridge History of the Cold War (The Cambridge History of the Cold War, pp. 267-288). Cambridge: Cambridge University Press. doi:10.1017/CHOL9780521837217.014

Reagan, R. 1983. Address to the nation on defence and national security. Retrieved from:
 http://www.atomicarchive.com/Docs/Missile/Starwars.shtml

Wittner, L. 2010. "Looking Back: The Nuclear Freeze and its Impact". Arms Control Today, 40(10), 53-56.

Westwick, P. 2008. "Space-Strike Weapons" and the Soviet Response to SDI. Diplomatic History, 32(5), 955-979. Retrieved May 12, 2020, from www.jstor.org/stable/24915966

Sagdeev, R. Z., & Garwin, R. 1994. The making of a Soviet scientist. Physics Today, 47(10), 69.

Pach, C. 2006. "The Reagan Doctrine: Principle, Pragmatism, and Policy". Presidential Studies Quarterly, 36: 75-88. doi:10.1111/j.1741-5705.2006.00288.x

Riedel, B. 2014. REAGAN AND CASEY. In What We Won: America's Secret War in Afghanistan, 1979–89 (pp. 110-127). Washington, D.C.: Brookings Institution Press. Retrieved May 13, 2020, from www.jstor.org/stable/10.7864/j.ctt6wpc21.10

National Security Council (NSC). 1985. The 1984 Boland Amendment, Brown University, Retrieved from: https://www.brown.edu/Research/Understanding_the_Iran_Contra_Affair/documents/d-nic-21.pdf

"Brezhnev Tried to Advance Moscow's Goals Through Detente Soviet Leader". 1982. The New York Times. Retrieved from: https://www.nytimes.com/1982/11/12/obituaries/brezhnev-tried-to-advance-moscow-s-goals-through-detente-soviet-leader.html

Gelb, H. 1984. Reagn's Foreign Policy Shifting Aim, The New York Times, Retrieved from: https://www.nytimes.com/1984/10/26/world/reagan-foreign-policy-shifting-aim.html

Brown University, Nicaragua and Iran Timeline(n.d.), Brown University, Retrieved from: https://www.brown.edu/Research/Understanding_the_Iran_Contra_Affair/timeline-n-i.php

Kindig, J. 2008. Anti-Nuclear organizing in the 1970s and 1980s, and Beyond. University of Washington. Retrieved from: https://depts.washington.edu/antiwar/pnwhistory_nukes.shtml

Beinart, P. 2010. Think again: Ronald Reagan, Foreign policy. Retrieved from: https://foreignpolicy.com/2010/06/07/think-again-ronald-reagan/

Clarke,J. (n.d.) Operation Urgent Furry: US Invasion of Grenada, United States Army, Retrieved from: https://history.army.mil/html/books/grenada/urgent_fury.pdf

Fischer, B. (n.d.) The Cold War Conundrum: The 1983 Soviet War Scares. CIA library, Retrieved from: https://www.cia.gov/library/center-for-the-study-of-intelligence/csi-publications/books-and-monographs/a-cold-war-conundrum/source.htm#HEADING1-12

Brown, A., & American Council of Learned Societies. 1997. The Gorbachev factor (ACLS Humanities E-Book (Series)). Oxford: Oxford University Press.

SIPRI yearbook. 2007. Armaments, disarmament and international security. (2008). Choice Reviews Online, 45(08), 675-690

Nincic, M. 1990. U. S. Soviet Policy and the Electoral Connection. World Politics, 42(3), 370-396. doi:10.2307/2010416

Pach, C. 2006. The Reagan Doctrine: Principle, Pragmatism, and Policy. Presidential Studies Quarterly, 36: 75-88. doi:10.1111/j.1741-5705.2006.00288.x

Matlock, J. 2004. Reagan and Gorbachev: How the Cold War ended (1st ed.), PP215-236, New York: Random House.

Wright, R. 2019. "The 1983 Beirut Barracks Bombing and the Current U.S. Retreat from Syria". *The New Yorker*. Retrieved from: https://www.newyorker.com/news/our-columnists/the-1983-beirut-barracks-bombing-and-the-current-us-retreat-from-syria

Acknowledgments

In writing this book we greatly benefited from the support of advice of numerous people, and would like to acknowledge them all. We would like to thank Armita Hosseini for her valuable contribution on the Iranian Revolution. Laura Maria Amaya Lamir, a wonderful editor who helped with the editing & publishing of this book. The following are acknowledgements by our individual authors.

I would like to thank my professor Dr. Ahmad Jachi for inspiring me to write and analyze such hot topics in his class—Special Topics during Financial Crises. Every lecture and every case study we worked on made me more aware and more passionate about what I was writing. I would also like to thank everyone who has believed in each and every word I have been writing since the start of my academic and professional career. Thank you Sophia and Tatios for everything.

Antranik Artinian

My parents have provided continual support since the beginning of the book writing project. My mother offered crucial assistance that enabled me to meet the deadline for this manuscript. My father kept me going with endless supplies of conversations and care. Thanks to Siddharth Sharma, who took me on the first publishing experience on the topic of Artificial Intelligence that made all of this possible.

Benjamin Ian Chen

Thank you, first and foremost, to my parents, Lilian and Daniel, for always cheering me on through every crazy project I've taken on during quarantine and comforting me when it all proved to be too much. Thank you also to my dearest friend Caroline for being my stability among so much uncertainty. You don't know how much your support and reassurance has meant to me. Thank you to every one of my friends who have directed kind words towards me this past year and to everyone at Youth Economist for allowing me to be part of this project, my fellow authors, and, of course, all of my writers at the Entrepreneurship section. Finally, I extend my acknowledgements to anyone who has hoped for brighter days for Latin America and has been part of every one of our hard fought accomplishments. I am moved and inspired by you.

Isabela de Almeida Godoy

Infinite thanks to my mother, Jessika, for being the only person who could understand me while I was writing like a possessed spirit and a special place for those who saw a writer in me way before the world recognized it.

Amy Espinoza Caldas

My grandfather, Iuda Dawid Goldman, has always supported and believed in me. He always pushed me to challenge myself and reach my full potential. I wanted to thank him for all the support and love!
I also wanted to thank my parents, Ana Paula and Alfredo, for allowing me to have the best education possible and to always insist that I continued studying and researching. A special thanks to my father who helped me in a brainstorm session when he suggested some of the topics I wrote about.

Júlia Felippe Goldman Vel Lejbman

I wish to express my gratitude to my parents E. Xu and Y. Bing for always being loving and supportive friends.

I would like to express my sincere appreciation for Dr. Pete Millwood and his amazing course on HY206 The International History of the Cold War which inspired my assessment on Reagan's foreign policy leading up to the collapse of the Soviet Union.

I also wish to thank the home department of my undergraduate degree where I was continuously inspired and challenged, in person or through zoom.

I hope you all may find my work to be an interesting read.

David Xu

About the Authors

Antranik Artinian currently is an economics undergraduate student at the Lebanese American University. He worked in Investopedia as a contributor and also takes part in Trivayu Infotech Incorporation as Management Associate.

Benjamin Ian Chen is an upcoming public policy and behavioral economics student at New York University. He is a research assistant at Harvard University Center for Geographic Analysis' reports, symposiums, and articles, and an employee at Kuomintang's Department of International Affairs, where he conducts research for national policy foundations.

Isabela de Almeida Godoy is a senior International Relations student from São Paulo, Brazil. She is the Director of the Entrepreneurship sector at the *Youth Politician* and focuses her efforts on the area of policymaking within a Latin American perspective. She is currently writing her thesis on public policies for the LGBTIQ+ Latin American populations after taking part in many international policymaking within a Latin American perspective. She also works as a Policy Brief Assistant with a network of women in academia aiming to empower women in politics in Brazil. Her goal now is to continue her path in public management and policy in hopes of creating safer and more just environments for social minorities everywhere.

Amy Espinoza Caldas is currently finishing her Bachelor's degree in Public Health at the University of the People. She has followed courses in Human Rights in Stanford University and the University of Geneva and she is certified in Digital Journalism by Reuters. Aside from her work as a political writer for the *Youth Economist* she writers for *Know all Sides*, *The Conference Corner* and *Lafflur*. She is devoted to bringing to life the stories of those who have been silenced.

Júlia Felippe Goldman Vel Lejbman is finishing her Bachelor's degree in International Relations at the Pontifical Catholic University of São Paulo, as well as Leisure and Tourism at the University of São Paulo. She is a IATI Community Platform Intern at UNDP, where she works closely with transparency and open data. Alongside working as a politics writer for the *Youth Economist*, she has been conducting, for the past two years, scientific research on the topics of foreign aid and development initiatives, particularly the case of the US aid to Central America's Northern Triangle. Júlia also has two podcasts, aimed at disseminating and democratizing knowledge. She is passionate about learning and, particularly, about making knowledge accessible to all.

David Xu recently completed his undergraduate degree with the department of international relations at the London School of Economics and Political Science. David will continue his master's study with the university this coming fall focusing on Media and Communication Governance. David is a staff writer of the security and intelligence division of the *Varemeng Journal*. He also works closely with the *Youth Economist* project

www.ingramcontent.com/pod-product-compliance
Lightning Source LLC
Chambersburg PA
CBHW031627210526
45464CB00004B/1778